Praise for
More

"I'm so thankful that as a young leader I was able to learn from Greg Hawkins. He taught me some of my earliest and most fundamental lessons—about leadership, about life, about faith—and I'm thrilled that now so many people will be able to learn from him through these pages. Greg is brilliant and kind, and his spiritual journey through these pages is a beautiful and inspiring one."

—SHAUNA NIEQUIST, author of *Bread & Wine* and *Savor*

"Greg Hawkins is a man with an enormously capable mind and a deeply feeling heart. His book *More* will help you connect your mind and heart to each other—and to God."

—JOHN ORTBERG, senior pastor, Menlo Church,
and author of *All the Places to Go*

"Greg Hawkins has given us all a gift. His transparency and humility invite us on a journey of discovery. *More* is a spiritual devotional derived from data gathered in the most technical way and then processed through the filters of a heartfelt search for God's best. Anyone who takes the time to read these pages can find hope and direction for the challenges life presents."

—ALLEN JACKSON, senior pastor, World Outreach Church

"I've had the privilege of working closely with Greg Hawkins for more than twenty years, and I've learned from experience that whenever Greg has something to say, I listen and learn! He is such an incredible student of God's work in us and in churches, and the *Reveal* study he led had a profound impact upon thousands of churches worldwide. Now he's taken it a step further in *More* to inspire and point us to the true living that God so passionately wants us to experience."

—SANTIAGO "JIMMY" MELLADO, president and CEO of
Compassion International and coauthor of *Small Matters*

"I enjoyed a front-row seat for two decades watching Greg yearn and reach for more. His spirit inspired me! This book will inspire you!"

—BILL HYBELS, senior pastor, Willow Creek Community
Church

"In Greg Hawkins's new book, *More,* he tackles the questions many of us have asked: 'Is there more to this life? Is there more to my relationship with God?' With very real conviction, he proves the answer is *yes!* Filled with practical, Scripture-based suggestions, years of research, and personal anecdotes, this book pushes us toward intimacy with God. I encourage anyone who wants to experience more of life to read this life-changing book."

—ROBERT MORRIS, founding senior pastor, Gateway
Church, and best-selling author of *The Blessed Life,*
Truly Free, and *Frequency*

"When I met Greg Hawkins more than twenty years ago, I quickly discovered his passion for Christ. Today he remains a person full of zeal and zest for living a Christian life of eternal significance—and his goal is to pass it on to you. *More* exemplifies how preparing in this life for the next life is the most important thing we as Christians can do. This book will grip your heart spiritually, as it did mine, and your soul will be stirred by Greg's vibrant faith and passion."

—JON R. WALLACE, president, Azusa Pacific University

"I've never read a book so data-driven that stirred my heart toward love in all my life. If you personally need a soul reawakening to long for and pursue more of the life Jesus promised, pick up *More* and don't be surprised when you struggle to put it down."

—SHANE FARMER, senior pastor, Cherry Hills Community
Church in Denver, CO

How to Move from Activity for God to Intimacy with God

MORE

God Has Everything
• Waiting for You

GREG L. HAWKINS

Foreword by Max Lucado

MULTNOMAH

Research data and analysis used by license from Originate Constructs.

Hardcover ISBN 978-1-60142-862-2
eBook ISBN 978-1-60142-863-9

Published in the United States by Multnomah, an imprint of the Crown Publishing Group, a division of Penguin Random House LLC, New York.

MULTNOMAH® and its mountain colophon are registered trademarks of Penguin Random House LLC.

Library of Congress Cataloging-in-Publication Data
Names: Hawkins, Greg L., author.
Title: More : how to move from activity for God to intimacy with God / Greg L. Hawkins.
Description: First Edition. | Colorado Springs, Colorado : Multnomah Books, 2016.
Identifiers: LCCN 2016010264 (print) | LCCN 2016016247 (ebook) | ISBN 9781601428622 (hardcover) | ISBN 9781601428639 (electronic)
Subjects: LCSH: Spirituality—Christianity. | Expectation (Psychology)—Religious aspects—Christianity.
Classification: LCC BV4501.3 .H3875 2016 (print) | LCC BV4501.3 (ebook) | DDC 248.4—dc23
LC record available at https://lccn.loc.gov/2016010264

Printed in the United States of America
2016—First Edition

10 9 8 7 6 5 4 3 2 1

To Lynn,
Forever and Always

Contents

The thief comes only to steal and kill and destroy; I have come that they may *have life,* and have it to the full.—Jesus

JOHN 10:10

Foreword

Greg Hawkins is a passionate man. When he talks, his eyes dance and his hands wave. When he listens, he leans forward and his eyes lock in. When he thinks, I promise, I hear gears whirring in his head. When he teaches, people listen, intently and joyfully. And when he talks about Jesus, oh, my goodness. When Greg talks about Jesus he is a groom describing his bride, an opera aficionado describing Puccini, a Green Bay Packers diehard retelling the glory days of Lombardi. When Greg talks about Jesus, he talks about the joy of his life.

That is why when Greg writes about *intimacy* with Jesus, we all need to perk up and take note. He gets it. And he longs for us to have it as well.

I love this book. It is an honor to applaud it. Greg tackles a fundamental question: the question of unmet expectations. How do we explain this disconnect in the hearts of many Christians? The faith they desire and the faith they experience are two different things. How can we span the gap between the cold faith of the status quo and the vibrant faith of the New Testament?

Greg addresses this question as only he can do. His research is unprecedented. He is a man of numbers and facts. He's unimpressed by hunches. He works off of solid evidence. You'll find it in these pages.

You'll also find practical solutions that emerge from three decades of church leadership. If you are looking for pie-in-the-sky suggestions, look elsewhere. If you want fact-based, Scripture-informed, ready-to-implement suggestions, this is your book and Greg is your guy.

This book is terrific for anyone who wants to grow in faith. Church leaders will find it to be an exceptional resource for strategizing. All Christians will find it to be a wonderful encouragement for spiritual growth. This is a powerful book, written by a wonderful man.

Prepare yourself to be encouraged.

Max Lucado

PART 1

CHAPTER 1

You know, it wasn't supposed to be this way."

It should have been a happy moment, and in many ways it was, until the truth set in. My fiancée, Lynn, and I were meeting with our pastor and friend Jim. We were with him for premarital counseling before our upcoming wedding and had talked about what marriage meant and what our expectations were for the marriage. Eventually the conversation turned to the ceremony itself.

We were going to be married in a charming 120-year-old Methodist church near my wife's hometown in the far west suburbs of Chicago. Jim would be sharing the responsibility of the service with the pastor of that church. As part of the discussion about the ceremony, Jim asked Lynn whom she had chosen to walk her down the aisle. Normally that's a fairly straightforward question, but Lynn's father had passed away nine years earlier when she was twenty. Lynn, without hesitation, calmly said, "No one."

"Certainly you have an uncle or family friend or a friend of yours who could walk you down the aisle?" he asked.

"No," she answered resolutely. "I'm going to walk by myself."

Jim tried one more time to talk her out of it, but she was adamant. "No, I'm going to go alone."

I'll never forget what happened next. Jim leaned forward, looked her square in the eye, and with a voice full of compassion said, "You know, it wasn't supposed to be this way."

In the silence that followed we all recognized the truth that was in the room, and we all started crying. Tears came down our faces, and we wept silently because what he said was so incredibly true. The three of us just sat in silence, letting the gravity of the statement sink in.

It really *wasn't* supposed to be this way. When she was a little girl she imagined this special day when she would walk down the aisle with her father proudly at her side. He was supposed to be there for the most important day of her life. It wasn't supposed to be this way.

Two months later when she turned the corner in the back of the church and started walking down the aisle looking stunningly beautiful, it became very clear to me, and to everyone else, that she was not walking alone—that her father in some way was very much with her. Her decision to walk by herself honored him so powerfully because his absence made us all aware of his presence. She had reserved that spot once and forever just for her father. No other man would ever take that place, ever. That day she paid tribute to all that her father had done for her, all the words of love, blessing, and belief he had conveyed to her in twenty short years. It was a beautiful thing yet painful at the same time.

It wasn't supposed to be this way.

That phrase hit me hard that day and has stayed with me for over twenty years. Its truth has extended beyond our marriage ceremony and caused me to reflect on how life itself was supposed to be. When I reflect on my own life—working at a marriage, having three children, doing my best to raise them right, getting up every day, going to work, working hard, being exhausted at some point every week, buying cars and homes, repairing roofs, paying bills, facing any number of struggles—I ask, is this how life was supposed to be?

Deep down in the private corners of our souls, we all ask that question, don't we? And if we're honest, most of us at one time or another feel that no, it wasn't supposed to be this way. Something is just a little, or a lot, off. Why are the relationships with the people I love the most so difficult? Why am I working harder and longer hours today than I did twenty years ago? Why do I struggle financially? Why didn't I get the promotion instead of the person with a whole lot less experience in the next office? Why did I get cancer, while others who seemingly neglect their bodies are cancer free? It seems that despite trying to do all the right things, life isn't turning out the way I thought it would.

Then I look at the world around us. The world in which our children will grow up. Conflicts and war, epidemics, terrorist attacks, collapsing economies, a giant gap between those who have and those who do not. It doesn't feel like God is winning at all. Is this really how it was supposed to be? I don't know about you, but too often I find myself thinking things will never get better in the world, which gives me an excuse to focus only on my own needs. Sure, I want a better life for everyone, but I can barely provide enough well-being for my own life, let alone do anything for the rest of the world.

Surely this is not the way it's supposed to be, right?

As a pastor, that question haunts me even more when it comes to matters of faith—for myself and for my congregation. When I look at all we do in the church—produce worship services, teach classes to the young and old, connect people in small groups, pray with those in need, organize serving experiences—I constantly wonder to myself, *Is this the way church is supposed to be?*

Think about your own experience. You go to church most Sundays (well, at least once a month). You pray. You read your Bible now and then. Maybe you're in a small group or even lead one. You volunteer to work with the children's ministry. Maybe you have gone on a mission trip to Guatemala. And all these things are good. Really good.

We do all these good things because we believe they will make us better people, give us better lives, bring us closer to God, and maybe even help others. And in many ways, they do. But if you are being honest with yourself, deep down, you want to believe there is more. You reflect on your relationship with God and wonder, *Is this how a relationship with God is supposed to feel?* And truthfully, you have gone beyond *wondering* if there is more to actually *wanting* more. And not just a little more. You want everything that Jesus promised when He said, "I have come that they may have life, and have it to the full" (John 10:10).

So you do all you know to do. You participate in even more activities at church or maybe look for a new church altogether. You find yourself spending more time in prayer and reading your Bible. And that seems to help, for a while. But then at some point, despite all that you are doing, you reach a plateau well short of your heart's desire. And you wonder all over again if this is all there is.

And then eventually, something awful happens. Little by little you start believing that more is not possible, and this is *exactly* how it was supposed to be. You convince yourself that good enough is, well, good enough. You remember that Jesus said, "In this world you will have trouble" (John 16:33) and resign yourself to the belief that the "full life" Jesus spoke about is not possible, nor intended, here on earth.

My sense is that some people get to this place in life and then, figuratively speaking, just hold their breath, hoping they have enough air to get to the very end. Hoping they can ignore their suspicion that there is more to life than what they are experiencing. They settle for the way things are, while they wait for their last real breath and ascension to heaven.

That's okay. I want to go to heaven too, but I'm not satisfied that earthly life for a Christian is just a long wait for heaven. I want more, and I want it now. And I think you do too.

I'm writing this book because I believe with all my being that each of us *can* experience the more that God has for us right here, right now. I don't have a magic formula or a set of ten easy steps that will improve your life. You've likely tried those and found them as hollow as I have. But in God's perfect timing and sovereignty, my own search for "more" coincided with some astonishing discoveries that came when a small team and I asked the Willow Creek Community Church congregation—and then over a thousand other congregations—to tell us the truth about their spiritual lives. It was not exactly the truth we were looking for, and it wasn't always easy to hear, but it created a profound shift in my thinking and has redirected the entire course of my life. I know more is possible right now, and on the following pages I will share with you what God has revealed to me through research, the Scriptures, and the stories of my friends about how a life of more actually works. Do I have it all figured out? No—and there is a real chance I have it all wrong. But I don't want to live any other way, and I suspect you don't either.

Despite the absence of Lynn's father at our wedding, it was a beautiful ceremony. She turned what could have been a reminder of his absence into a tribute to the special place he occupies in her life. It wasn't easy for her, and she would be the first to say she would have rather not walked alone down the aisle. But she made do. We all do. We've learned that when things don't work out the way we hoped, we make the best of it, and usually that's a good thing. Except where God is concerned. He did not invite us into a relationship so that we could just make do but so that we could experience *more*.

It took me a long time to learn that.

REFLECT

> You let the world, which doesn't know the first thing
> about living, tell you how to live. (Ephesians 2:2, MSG)

On a scale of 1 (very unsatisfied) to 10 (very satisfied), how satisfied
are you with your life right now? Does it feel like you are living a
full life or just a busy one?

CHAPTER 2

A Search
for More

grew up in Port Arthur, Texas. It's a small town famous for having more oil refining capacity than anywhere outside of Saudi Arabia. I still haven't gotten the smell of petrochemicals out of my nose. For the longest time, I thought that was what *air* smelled like—a mixture of jet fuel and burning. But as I now know, that is not how air is supposed to smell.

My parents, Skip and Joyce, provided a safe and loving environment for me and my two brothers and sister. For that, I am grateful. As a kid, I loved to ride my bike, fly kites, eat snow cones, and climb tall trees. But my true love was building and launching rockets into the sky. The higher, the better. I was fortunate to grow up in the era of the Apollo missions. Neil Armstrong stepped on the moon just days shy of my seventh birthday. In that way, I was like many kids my age—fascinated by the new frontier of our country's space program. But in other ways, I was quite different.

It had to do with how we grew up. My father, you see, loved music. Every night, he would put a record on our stereo and crank up the music in our little East Texas home. You might guess bluegrass or country or rock. Nope. Opera.

We would sit at our family dinner table and play Name That

Tune—with opera. We'd try to name the opera and the composer. If we could name the act that particular selection was from, we got bonus points. We actually would get a quarter for each correct answer, so there were fairly high stakes for opera trivia at that point.

I loved opera. It moved me. As a child as young as four, I would listen to incredible pieces of music played really loudly, mostly sung in Italian, some in German. I could not understand the words, but I could feel the emotion and power. I would be so moved by certain pieces of music I would start to cry.

The beauty of the music and the longing in the voices touched me. I was embarrassed by my tears, so I would hide behind the couch or a chair, or just outside of the room, because I didn't want my family to see me crying. Music was never a mere distraction. It was something profound and mysterious, a very real gift to my soul, both then and now.

As I grew up, I learned the stories behind the screaming Italian voices—stories of desire, pain, victory. My favorite opera was (and still is) *Turandot,* written by the great Italian composer Giacomo Puccini in 1924. Set in the Forbidden City in Beijing, China, hundreds of years ago, it tells the tale of Turandot, the royal princess with an ice-cold heart. To vet all potential husbands, a contest was created. Answer three riddles correctly and you can marry her. Miss just one and off with your head.

Enter Calaf, a prince in exile, who sees Turandot and is immediately consumed by her beauty. Act 1 ends as he bangs a massive gong announcing his intentions to face the riddles. In Act 2 he successfully answers the questions, but Turandot is not so happy about it all. Being a good sport, Calaf (who has gone unnamed up to this point) offers her a way out: "You gave me three riddles; I will give you one," he says. "If you can discover my name by sunup then the deal is off and my head along with it."

Act 3 opens with one of the most beautiful and recognizable arias in opera, the "Nessun Dorma" sung by Calaf, where he declares early the next day before sunup, *Vincero! Vincero!"* which means "I shall win! I shall win!" Turandot's advisors show up trying to bribe Calaf with wealth and other women, but he refuses. Eventually they drag in his father and his servant Liu, threatening to torture them. Liu steps forward declaring she is the only one who knows his name, declares her undying love for Calaf, and drives a dagger into her own heart to prevent herself from spilling the beans. Liu's act of sacrifice begins to melt Turandot's heart.

However, Calaf does not want Turandot to marry him out of obligation. So he privately tells her his name, even though it will mean his certain death. Turandot, with Calaf at her side, triumphantly announces to her father, the emperor, in front of all the townspeople that she knows the stranger's name. "His name," she says, "is . . ."

I'll tell you what she said in just a minute.

One day I found myself home alone, listening to *Turandot*. The stereo was cranked about as loud as it would go, which is really the only way to listen to opera. I was seventeen, approaching the end of high school, and contemplating my future. Looking back now I understand that I had become a fairly depressed young man at that point. I didn't really understand life. I didn't understand the goal. I was confused, and in some ways life felt purposeless but also frightening. My Christian faith talked about a loving God and this great abundant life that was available. But I looked at the lives of the adults in my life (and in my church), and they didn't seem to be experiencing that kind of life. I couldn't reconcile the difference. I didn't know much, but I knew that was not how life was supposed to be. There had to be more.

So there I was, alone, listening to opera, and at the very end Turandot announces his name, and then the townspeople go wild screaming and the music crescendos to the very majestic ending. As usual, I was moved to tears. But although I'd heard the opera many times before and knew the general story line, and could feel the intense emotion, I didn't know what they were saying. I didn't speak Italian.

I pulled out the libretto, which translates the Italian to English, and I read the very last scenes where Turandot goes before her father and announces proudly, "Father, I know the stranger's name." She says, "His name is . . ." and there is a pause. Then she proudly announces, "His name is Love!" She doesn't rat him out, yet she gives his true name. His name is Love.

I broke down, reading those words, but then I continued reading. The celebratory outcry of the people—what were they saying? They responded to her proclamation, sounding like an angelic chorus, exclaiming, "Love! Light of the world . . . glory to thee! Glory! Glory!" and the opera ends. I was seventeen, and I was undone.

CALLED TO LOVE

In that moment God met me in a very powerful way. He made two things very clear to me. First, all of life, *everything,* is all about love. God's true identity is love Himself: His name is love, He is love, and the most important thing in life is to love Him. Also in that moment, God made it clear to me that the second most important thing in life is people and that my goal, my job for the rest of my life, is to love them. I am called to love (see Matthew 22:36–39; Mark 12:29–31).

Now I didn't respond like some sort of Texas teenage version of Mother Teresa, rejoicing over this wonderful revelation. In fact, I didn't like what I had just realized because people for the most part scared me, hurt me, and confused me. I didn't understand how they operated: one minute acting one way, the next acting another way. I just didn't get it. To think that I was going to go out of my way to love them, to extend myself for them, seemed like a terrifying idea.

In that moment God gave me a picture to go with those words, a picture that calmed and helped me. I saw in my imagination a group of about two dozen men and women whom I had never met, standing in a circle, holding hands, and looking inward.

At the center of the circle, I saw myself. I was staring at all these people, feeling unconnected and unwilling to join in the circle. I saw myself walking toward the edge of the circle, fully intending to walk right past them out of the circle. I really was at a turning point in my life where I was about to walk away from people and decide that my path in life going forward was not going to include them. I would figure out life on my own. I walked to the edge of that circle and broke the circle by separating two people holding hands. But as I started to step past them, I felt God saying *no*. At that moment I turned around and joined the hands I had just separated. I looked at the faces of the people in the circle, and in that moment I knew this would be the picture that would guide the rest of my life.

I knew from that point on that my job was to love people. Not because I needed them but because God asked me to, because they mattered to Him. People are the crowning achievement of His creation, and they were the reason He sent His Son. Again, this was not something that was easy for me, and it was not something I wanted to do. On that day I made a profound choice to trust God in spite of my anxiety and fear. In that choice, a shift occurred inside my head and inside my heart. Love is a choice, and people are the only things that matter.

WHAT DOES LOVE LOOK LIKE?

That moment was a turning point in my life. We all have them: moments where suddenly things just shift, and you can't go back to seeing things the way you did before.

Now, being called to love is one thing. But how do you do that? What does love look like? We all ask this question, and it's the question that drives us to search for a life of more. We know we're supposed to love God and love people—the two things Jesus said were most important. But how, exactly, do we love? You may or may not have had an experience like the one I've just shared, but I know you've asked these questions: Is this how life is supposed to be? Is there more to life? And because we sense that there is, we ask, How do we get there? From that moment on, I was on a journey to figure that out. When I look back, I can see how God was guiding me. But most of the time, probably like you, I felt like my life unfolded more by chance than by any plan or strategy.

As college loomed, I had no idea what career to pursue or even where to go to college. I ended up at Texas A&M University, studying civil engineering, with the idea that perhaps I'd become an architect. Through my involvement in student leadership it became clear that working with people was more interesting to me than designing buildings, so I set my sights on a business career. After college and two years of work, I moved to California and got my MBA from Stanford University.

Nearing the end of graduate school, I still had no clarity about what job I should take. But God eventually made a path clear, a path I never saw coming. A path that required this Texan to move to a northern city. Why would He send a warm-weather guy who likes working with people to a snowy, cold city where I knew next to no one? Chicago? Really, God?

A Very Large Church in the Suburbs

So I moved to Chicago to work as a management consultant, and as I did with every other move, I began looking for a church. After about a year of visiting a variety of churches, a friend told me about a very large church in the suburbs called Willow Creek Community Church. Even as I drove into the parking lot it was clear to me that this wasn't your ordinary neighborhood church. It looked more like a corporate headquarters.

I finally found my way to an auditorium and slipped into a seat toward the back. A large stage stretched across the front where a group of musicians led the congregation in contemporary worship music—this was *not* the Lutheran church of my childhood. Then the senior pastor, Bill Hybels, walked onstage. During his sermon, he said something that stopped me in my tracks: "Ninety percent devotion to Christ is 10 percent too little."

My whole mind lit up, and I realized I'd been waiting my entire life for somebody to say that. In some ways it was like someone turned on a switch inside of me and helped me understand that maybe life *was* supposed to be different. Certainly my faith was supposed to be different. And if that happened, maybe my whole life could be different. The *more* I was looking for might actually be possible. That was all I needed to hear; I started attending Willow Creek.

In the last few months of 1990, I was at a point in my career where continued advancement would mean even longer hours, more days of travel, and more weekends. I was single, and at the rate I was going I would stay that way with this kind of lifestyle. And then my body told me to slow down, with a bout of stress-induced shingles at the age of twenty-seven. Something had to change.

I went home to visit my parents in Texas for some vacation time around the Christmas holidays. While I was there, I did some soul searching. *What do I really want? Where will my continued pursuit of career success take me, and do I really want to go there?* I had lunch with my former pastor who told me some crazy thing about how he knew I would end up working for a church. I just shook my head. But after a few days of prayer and reflection, I got some clarity about what really mattered to me. Being a business guy, I wrote a personal mission statement based on my discoveries: my life would be about empowering people to build Christian community.

I had no idea of the full implications of that statement, and some of it surprised me. But it seemed clear that I shouldn't continue as a management consultant. I decided to leave my job, to stay in Chicago to be more involved at Willow Creek, and to find a job where I didn't have to get on an airplane every Monday. I had a year's worth of living expenses saved, which I believed would give me time to find the right next job. But more than that, as I flew back to Chicago a few days later, I hoped that whatever was next would help me discover life as it was meant to be.

I left my job in early March. Within a few days, out of the blue, I was invited to have lunch with one of Willow Creek's teaching pastors, Jim Dethmer.

Jim told me that although Willow was growing, many people were also leaving because they couldn't get connected. The leaders of the church had asked him to build a church-wide system where everyone in the church would be in a small group, led by trained and empowered leaders. "We're going to empower people to build Christian community," he said.

I was speechless. He had just echoed back my mission statement, which I'd written the week before. And without skipping a beat, he continued, "Why don't you take a year off and come help me build it?" He paused. "And we don't have money to pay you, but it seems that you don't need the money anyway." On the spot, without thinking for another second, I said, "Yes."

Now, that might seem like a big leap to you, but it was no leap at all. It completely lined up with my mission statement. And after all, it was for only one year. But deep down, I really hoped that this would be the beginning of finding why God had put me here on earth. That maybe this would fill the longing in my soul for more. More life. More purpose.

After that fun and challenging year, I was asked to stay on (with pay, thankfully) to help further develop the new ministry and to assist with redesign of the church's membership process. Then in 1994, Bill Hybels asked me to help the leadership of Willow Creek develop a strategic plan. I completed that work at the end of 1995, and I was ready to move on. But then Hybels asked me to join the leadership team, become executive pastor, and essentially be responsible for running the day-to-day operations of the church.

That took me completely by surprise. Part of me thought, *Okay, maybe this is what I'm supposed to do with my life.* It may have taken thirty years, but I now felt as if my life might actually make some sense. I was part of a great church. I had an interesting job. I had married an amazing woman—my wife, Lynn, whom I met at Willow. Life was good, I thought. This would all work out just fine. Maybe this is how it was supposed to be. The answer to my question, the search for life as it is supposed to be, seemed to be this: this job, this church, this life.

So I threw myself into my work.

Is Bigger Better?

Church attendance grew. My responsibilities included leading a $50 million capital campaign to build a new, larger auditorium and start regional campuses all over the Chicago area. We were a very large church and had big plans to become even larger. Which was a good thing, right? We were expanding God's kingdom, right?

Life for me was finally the way it was supposed to be. Well, sort of. The questions were no longer at the surface, but before long they bubbled up. It was, in some ways, like trying to hold a beachball under the water.

In 2002, the reality of managing Willow's growth hit me square in the gut: we had to lay off thirty-two people, the first time the church ever had to lay off anyone. A large part of this was due to the economic downturn that began that year, but part of it was also my responsibility—because of some decisions I made. While those decisions had the support of our leadership team, I put a lot of the blame on myself. Suddenly, ministry wasn't as much fun.

In the wake of that experience, these questions haunted me: Is any of this work I'm doing making a real difference? Are the successes we've experienced—the growth, the small groups, the service projects—making a tangible difference in the world and in people's lives or just making us all feel better? Does attending church, joining a Bible study, volunteering, or even going on a mission trip get me closer to God? Does it make me act more like Jesus? The bottom line was this: Does my religious activity make me more loving?

I asked myself, *What if someone wants to donate $100,000 to our church, stipulating only that it be used where it would make the most difference in people's lives? Would we know what to do with that generous donation? Do we really know what programs or projects we should be investing in as a church?* As a leader, that haunted me.

When I'd drive onto our church parking lot and watch the construction of the new auditorium progressing, when I'd look over financial reports at how much this huge building was costing us, I kept asking myself, *Is this the right way to do things?* I would look at that huge construction site that would soon be our auditorium, steel girders seeming to grow overnight on their own, and wrestle with doubt (and feel guilty even asking the questions): Would bigger buildings and more locations really help people grow? Would more building mean more life change? More *life*? Life to the full?

Where should a church direct its resources if it really wants to help its members grow closer to God? If it isn't in bigger buildings and more innovative programs, where is it? Eventually, I wasn't the only one asking these questions. Our staff was wrestling with them as well.

The answer came from the most unlikely place.

What's Working (and What's Not)?

In the fall of 2003, as our church was asking these questions and watching the very large building addition take shape before their eyes, a small miracle occurred. It changed the trajectory of our church and my life.

Cally Parkinson, Willow Creek's communications director, introduced me to Eric Arnson, a market research expert she had worked with prior to coming to Willow. Eric's cutting-edge firm studied consumers, but not just in terms of income, age, career, or other typical demographics. Instead, his firm got inside the hearts and minds of consumers to truly understand their attitudes, wants, needs, and desires. He'd used those insights to help clients like Nike, John Deere, Gatorade, The Weather Channel, and Levi Strauss & Co.

When we met, I shared with him my concerns. We were crystal clear about our goal. We were committed to living out the charge Jesus gave His followers right before He ascended into heaven: "Go and make disciples of all the nations . . ." (Matthew 28:19, NLT). We believed disciples were people characterized by their love of others and their increasing love and devotion to God. Jesus said, "By this everyone will know that you are my disciples, if you love one another" (John 13:35).

I told Eric our strategy was to get people participating in a variety of activities at church, and we believed that increased participation in church activities over time would lead to spiritual growth. Or as we sometimes said: Church Activity = Spiritual Growth = Loving People.

How Most People Think About Spiritual Growth

services
retreats small group
short-term missions
worship evangelism
sunday classes
serving Bible study

A person far from God participates in church activities, which produce a person who loves God and loves others.

I know I'm biased, but I thought we did as good a job as any church—maybe better than some—at getting people actively engaged. People didn't just show up on weekends for a worship service but regularly participated in small groups, volunteered in the many service opportunities we provided, and took advantage of all sorts of classes and programs designed to help them grow in their faith. Every program and activity was aimed at helping people become *fully devoted followers of Jesus*. We wanted to help them grow into 100 percent commitment.

But the problem was, I explained, we didn't know which, of all the hundreds of programs we offered, were helping them become more loving. And we couldn't keep funding all those programs. The truth was we really didn't know how to measure our effectiveness.

Eric told us that he could help us discover what catalyzes increasing levels of love toward others and toward God. I had my doubts. Serious doubts. We'd been doing church at Willow Creek for nearly thirty years and this guy had almost no church experience, other than attending a small Episcopal church in his hometown. How could he provide us with new insights? But we decided to move forward with Eric, especially since he offered to do all this for free. He called in a lot of favors, recruiting his friends and former colleagues to join members of our staff in a one-of-a-kind research project that, according to him, would tell us what worked and what didn't.

We jumped in. We read everything we could find on how spiritual development works and then interviewed over one hundred

Willow attendees to learn about their spiritual lives. The project eventually mushroomed, and by the time we were finished, over nine thousand folks from our church had taken a survey designed by Eric and the team. We could hardly wait to see the results. We each had our own hunches as to what activities really were the most effective. So you can imagine how eager we were when he called to say he had analyzed all the responses and wanted to meet to go over the findings. And you can imagine how I felt when I heard the first line of his summary:

"All of your assumptions about what you're doing are *wrong*."

Reflect

> Keep on asking, and you will receive what you ask for.
> Keep on seeking, and you will find. Keep on knock-
> ing, and the door will be opened to you. For everyone
> who asks, receives. Everyone who seeks, finds. And to
> everyone who knocks, the door will be opened.
> (Matthew 7:7–8, NLT)

What are you asking God for these days? Or put another way, what are the desires of your heart? Be as specific as you can.

Bonus: On YouTube at www.youtube.com/watch?v=rTFUM4Uh _6Y, watch one of the greatest tenors of all time, Luciano Pavarotti, sing "Nessun Dorma." This 1994 clip is particularly good. It doesn't matter that you probably don't know what he is saying; just know that his last word, *Vincero,* means "I will win."

At the end of your life, what do you want more than anything else and would be willing to declare with as much passion and strength as Pavarotti?

CHAPTER 3

The Stunning Breakthrough

W*rong? Our assumptions are all wrong? What?*

"You asked me to help you discover which activities created the greatest spiritual growth," Eric began. "But the data told us that involvement in church activities does not predict greater spiritual growth. We found people who aren't very involved at Willow who have a deep love for others and God, and we found people who are very much involved in everything your church offers whose lives are not characterized by love. And vice versa. Simply put, involvement in stuff at your church just does not predict someone's love of God or love of others."

Looking at our shocked expressions, he tried to offer a bit of encouragement: "We did see some movement as people went from low to high involvement, but it is tiny. I think we are looking at this all wrong."

I rapidly cycled through three reactions. First, that helped explain why I was so tired. We had to get people involved in *everything* at church, just to see any movement in their hearts. That took a lot of work. Second, I thought perhaps we were just ineffective. Maybe other churches had better or different results. But while I knew we had room to improve, I also knew we did things really well, so much so that thousands of church leaders visited Willow each year to learn how we did things. The third thought, which came so quickly it surprised me, was the possibility that our activity-based strategy for spiritual growth was all wrong, like Eric suggested.

Eric asked for more time to make sense of the data, which I gladly gave him, since at that point I didn't know what to think or how to behave as a leader in a local church. We now knew what didn't work: church activity did not lead to intimacy with God or to becoming a more loving person. But what did move people closer to God? Six weeks later Eric returned with the bold declaration: "I think we found something!"

Eric told us that how long someone had been a Christian didn't matter. Age, gender, church attendance since childhood—all that didn't matter. But what did? A single question on the survey, which simply asked, "How important is Jesus to you?" That one question enabled the researchers to group the congregation into four very distinct groups.

Four Groups

In Group 1 are people who for the most part believe in God but are unsure about Jesus. Their relationship with God is impersonal. Some of them are actively seeking God or investigating the claims of Jesus, while others have stopped their active pursuit yet continue to show up at church, simply going through the motions. So they could be actively seeking or stagnant. They might typically describe themselves in this way: "I believe in God, but I am not sure about Jesus. My faith is not a significant part of my life."

In Group 2 are people who do believe that Jesus is God's Son and who are working on what that means for their lives. Their relationship with Jesus has become personal but not close. Most of them would say, "I believe in Jesus and am trying to figure out what it means to get to know Him."

In Group 3 are folks who have a close relationship with Jesus in which they look to Him for help, comfort, and direction. They have chosen to have Him influence their daily lives. They might describe themselves by saying, "I feel really close to Jesus and depend on Him daily for guidance." That sounded good to me. I wanted people in our church to get to that place.

"However," Eric continued, "there is one more group."

Group 4 includes people who describe their relationship with Jesus as the most important relationship in their lives and say that it defines everything they think and do. The big difference between Group 3 and Group 4 is that to the people in Group 3 Jesus is important to their lives, but the focus is still on *their* lives, while Group 4 people have decided that their own lives don't truly matter. Christ has become the center of their lives. They have set aside the agendas for their lives and are attempting to live for God.

So far, so good. Eric and the team could place people into four groups. Okay, so now what? Well, things got very interesting when Eric next showed us graph after graph that showed *every single measure* of love of others and love of God increased dramatically up and

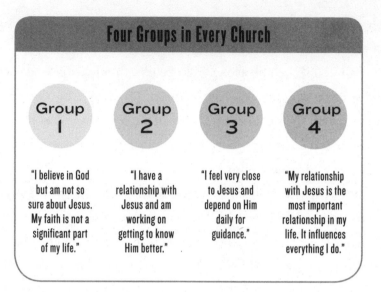

to the right as you went from Group 1 all the way to Group 4. It was crazy. Group 4 people served others, shared their faith, were generous with their resources, and had higher levels of peace, patience, and joy.

After seeing well over forty different graphs, there was one unmistakable conclusion. Spiritual growth, the process of becoming a more loving person, was not about increasing participation in church activities. Spiritual growth was about increasing intimacy with Christ. Intimacy, not activity. Loud and clear.

All of this started to make sense and I was really motivated to help the members of the church become part of Group 4, but I still needed to know which church programs should be funded and which ones should be downsized or eliminated. I asked Eric if the team had any insights into the question. He said in order to answer that question, we would need to understand what helped someone move from Group 1 to Group 2, Group 2 to Group 3, and Group 3 to Group 4, and he believed that the data could give us insights. Over the next many months, and then the next decade, as the research expanded to include more than half a million people in over two thousand churches, a picture of how people move from Group 1 all the way to Group 4 emerged.

We started making adjustments to our church's programs and budget in response to what we were learning. And because we had data from thousands of other churches, we started to learn what some of the more spiritually vibrant churches were doing to help their people move toward greater intimacy with God, helping us further refine our strategies and programs.

This was all very exciting, both at our church and among the churches who graciously let us survey their congregations. Eventually, Cally Parkinson and I wrote a few books for church leaders about what we had learned, culminating with the book *Move: What 1,000 Churches Reveal About Spiritual Growth.*

But this is not a book about all of that.

LONGING FOR MORE

You see, over the past twelve years, this has become very personal to me. I thought that all God was asking from me was to be a better leader of a local church, and as a bonus, He was asking me to share what I was learning with other church leaders. Simple enough.

But every time I talked with pastors about what people really needed and wanted from their churches and how they could make some changes, I turned into a crazy man. I would plead with them, jumping up and down if necessary. This was not a sterile, data-driven experiment for me. This was personal.

It might sound a bit weird, but I felt (and still feel) a responsibility to the five hundred thousand people who told us about their spiritual lives. I didn't want that responsibility, but it was there. I tried to get rid of it, but it wouldn't leave. I can't get them (you) out of my head or off my heart.

And the one thing they were saying loud and clear to those of us in church leadership is this: "We Want More!" More from church and more of God.

One of the fascinating and a bit controversial parts of the research dealt with asking people how satisfied they were with their church. I know this sounds awful and very consumer focused, but we asked them questions like "How satisfied are you with how your church is helping you grow spiritually?" We didn't ask them if the music was too loud, too hip, or too boring. We didn't ask them if they liked the pastor and the rest of the staff. We wanted to know how the church and its programs were helping them grow *spiritually*.

Now, before I go further, you need to understand how people answer a question like that. Satisfaction is really about met or unmet expectations and desires. In almost every experience or situation in our lives, we bring a set of expectations. We go to a new restaurant. If the food, service, and atmosphere meet our expectations, then we say we are "satisfied." Simply satisfied. But if any or all parts of the experience go beyond our expectations, then we say we are "very or extremely satisfied." And if we have bad food, rude service, and the whole place smells like old fish, then we are "dissatisfied or very dissatisfied." Satisfaction is relative to what we are expecting or wanting. When studying satisfaction, all you really want to look at are those who say they are extremely or very satisfied. That gives you the information you need to know if you are really serving a customer or helping someone move closer to God.

The results of the "how satisfied are you" question surprised us. Forty-one percent of everyone in Group 1, across all churches, said they were extremely or very satisfied with their church. That went up to 52 percent for Group 2 and then plateaued at 58 percent for Groups 3 and 4. Let that sink in. Does 58 percent sound high or low to you?

Well, it sounds entirely too low to me. That would be like getting a three out of five on a Yelp review. Would that be a restaurant you would want to go to? Probably not. But here is the deal: you can't judge that answer until you know what people want from their church. Remember, satisfaction is all about met or unmet expectations or desires. So what do people want from their church?

We gave the people we surveyed a very long list of all the things they could want from their church, and here is what they said was most important to them, in rank order:

1. Help me understand the Bible in greater depth.
2. Help me develop a personal relationship with Christ.

3. Give me church leaders who model and reinforce how I can grow spiritually.

4. Challenge me to grow and take the next steps.

Perhaps if you think about your own church experience, these longings resonate with you. They reflect what you want from your church as well. What emerges is a picture of people who want *more.* They want more understanding of the Bible. They want a deeper, more personal relationship with Christ. They want to be challenged to grow, and they want their leaders to be the ones showing them what to do and how to do it. Sounds reasonable to me. In fact, what they *want* is exactly what they *need* to grow closer to Jesus, based on the research.

And if you read between the lines, what they are really asking for is more of God. They want to know Him more. To be closer to Him. To be more personal. And they want to grow and change and are giving church leaders permission to teach and challenge and model how that all works.

People want more from their church and more from God.

So am I saying we all should be looking for the perfect church that meets all our needs? Well, no. Now, there are churches that seem to help meet those needs better than others. That's true. But what is equally true is that the "more" people are longing for is available whether you are in a good church or a struggling church. Remember, we learned that drawing closer to God is not about all the fancy programs at a church. Those programs can help, but participating in them does not predict whether you will draw closer to God.

What I am suggesting is that the "more" you are longing for from your church and from God is available, *regardless of the church you attend.* I can say that with confidence because we discovered, in the data, a group of people living a life of more, regardless of how well their church was helping them grow spiritually.

More Is Possible

Over the past decade I have been particularly drawn to the folks in Group 4, wanting to understand how they arrived at their decision to lay down their lives to follow God completely. Truth be told, I wanted to understand them because I wanted to be like them.

As we dug deeper in the data, we discovered that within Group 4 there was a subset of people who were even more intimate with God. These folks represented about half of Group 4, which translates to about 12 percent of all the people in the churches we surveyed. It's not just like one or two people in a church. Twelve percent is around one out of eight. So one out of eight people in a given church, statistically, was in this group. When we isolated their responses to the survey questions, their responses were not only a little bit different; they were remarkably different. Truly these folks were a group living a life of more.

This group seized my imagination. Here was a group of people who most strongly resonated with the statement "Christ is the center of my life. My relationship with Him is the most important relationship in my life. Every decision I make is connected with that relationship."

These people are not to be admired only for their commitment to Christ. What is compelling about them is that they are the group who reports the highest levels of love for God, and, less predictably, they exhibit the fruit of the Spirit (love, joy, peace, patience, and so on) in measurably greater amounts than any other group. Even though they have set aside their own agendas, their own lives, they are the most satisfied and fulfilled. They are living proof of Jesus's words: if you want to gain your life, you must lose it (see Matthew 16:25).

These people experience intimacy with Christ rather than just being involved in activities for God. Although they might appear to engage in the same activities and actions, their motivations are completely different.

They spend more time in the Bible, not out of obligation, but because they can't get enough of God and His Word. Their hearts are broken by the pain they see in the world around them, not merely out of sympathy, but from a deep love they have for others. They don't do this perfectly or all the time. However, as their intimacy with God increases, their motives and attitudes are transformed.

Folks in this group have more purpose. They understand why they're here on earth. They understand that they have spiritual gifts and are focused on making a real difference in the world. They are open to what God wants them to do. They believe that they're made for a purpose and they're pursuing it.

Finally, what's incredibly clear is that folks in this Group 4 subset exhibit more love. They have tremendous love for people they know and those they don't know. More than double the number of those in Group 3. They're willing to put others first even if they don't know them. They're able to forgive others regardless of whether those people ask for forgiveness. They're willing to love unconditionally and forget and forgive. In moments of disappointment with others they are still willing to love and serve and pray for them.

More love, more peace, more purpose. If you saw a few people like that in your church, you might assume they are outliers, people who are unusual, perhaps gifted. But we have seen tens of thousands of people like this from all across the country, from all different churches, from all different ethnicities and ages. It's the *more* that you desire for your own life.

People in this group love God with their whole heart and love others as themselves. They have found a life of purpose, a life of loving others, a life of inner contentment and peace. We want these things. We crave that kind of life, especially when we learn that it's not about *doing* more things.

The good news is that you can have this kind of life. You can find the more you're looking for.

Jesus once said, "This is what the kingdom of God is like. A man scatters seed on the ground. Night and day, whether he sleeps or gets up, the seed sprouts and grows, though he does not know how"

(Mark 4:26–27). *He does not know how.* There is something about the spiritual growth process that is completely mysterious. There is no formula for moving into being fully intimate with God, but after spending almost a decade trying to understand this through the lens of research, reflecting on the words of Scripture, and reflecting on my own life, I've come to conclude there are some patterns, some essential shifts in thought and action that people in this group have made. They have not launched a self-improvement plan but have been changed by their deep desire for more of God.

Before I describe those shifts, we need to go back. Way back to the very beginning to understand how life was supposed to be.

REFLECT

> One thing I ask from the LORD,
>   this only do I seek:
> that I may dwell in the house of the LORD
>   all the days of my life,
> to gaze on the beauty of the LORD
>   and to seek him in his temple. (Psalm 27:4)

Think about the people closest to you, the ones you love the most—spouse, children, friends. How do you currently feel about them? Close or distanced? What do they mean to your life? Then think about Jesus. How close do you feel to Him? Do you want to get closer, or are you happy where you are?

CHAPTER 4

The Way It's
Supposed to Be

W e were created for deep intimacy and oneness with God. By "created for," I don't just mean some sort of unattainable ideal. It's what Adam and Eve actually experienced in the beginning—a joyful dependency and trust. Our rebellion against God was not simply eating a forbidden fruit but also rejecting God's authority and provision. We did not want to be dependent on Him; we wanted to be our own bosses, our own gods, our own kings and queens.

Unfortunately, having our own way doesn't always work out as well as we might hope. But the story of God and His people doesn't end with the Fall. It goes on to redemption and restoration. We can have that deep intimacy and oneness that we were originally created to experience. In fact, that is what God wants to give us, what He can give us right now.

He wants us to be a part of His kingdom.

We were made for an intimacy we cannot even imagine, one in which we feel loved and safe and joyful in ways we've never experienced in this life. We might experience moments of joy or meaning or intimacy with God, say, during a particularly meaningful worship service, a moment alone with God, a time when we see something beautiful in nature, or maybe even while serving on a mission trip. When we get a little taste, or a glimpse, of the kingdom of God, it makes us want more of Him.

The problem is, as wonderful as the momentary glimpses of God are, as comforting as those fleeting moments of the assurance of His love can be, we like being our own bosses. We want those wonderful feelings of intimacy with God, but we don't want anyone telling us what to do. It's not that we have anything against God. We just don't like the idea of Him (or anyone) being king. We don't want anyone, even God, to be the boss of us. We want to be our own kings and queens and build our own kingdoms. At the same time, we want to feel God's love and presence. However, we can't have it both ways.

In our more honest moments, we know that our tendencies to want to do things our own way, to be selfish or self-centered, are just a part of who we are, and we also know that our self-focus keeps us from experiencing intimacy with God. After all, those moments of intimacy we occasionally experience happen when we take the focus off of ourselves.

Still, letting go of ourselves, our agendas, our kingdoms is a scary idea. So instead of embracing our design as a creation by a Creator, instead of enjoying God's protection and provision and rule as our King, we become little kings and queens of our own little kingdoms, believing that we can make it on our own and that our lives would be better if we could be in charge. We think if we're the bosses, life will be great. But it isn't. Life on our own is very difficult.

Most of us live in our own kingdoms. We rule the "Kingdom of

Me." It sounds great at first. However, it is not easy running your own kingdom. In fact, it's a lot of hard work. We have to provide and protect—that's what kings and queens do. We have to find ways to resource our kingdoms because we need things like groceries, clothing, health insurance, cell phone plans, and the Internet. God's original plan was that we would live in His kingdom and He would take care of all that. But now that we are kings and queens of our own kingdoms, we have to work hard and pay our bills and save up for retirement. And for some reason, we always seem to need more stuff.

There's just never enough stuff in our kingdoms.

It's (Not So) Good to Be King

Most of us want to rule over good kingdoms, so we do our best to treat others well and live ethically. What we're really looking for is meaning and purpose, but that's not always easy. When it's "our life" and God is just our "help," then the job of protecting and providing is still up to us. That's a lot of pressure   and it's a job God never intended us to shoulder.

When we are focused on protecting and providing for our own kingdoms, everyone else seems like a threat. If people seem at all unfriendly or threatening, we protect ourselves by trying to keep them out. If others seem to have more provisions, we get upset because that just seems unfair. So we work harder and try to acquire more so that our kingdoms have as much as theirs. We tend to measure kingdom success by standards imposed by other people: How much stuff do we have, and how good is our stuff compared to the stuff of other people? But because we're working so hard to get all that stuff, we never have any time to enjoy it.

After working so hard to keep our kingdoms running, we finally reach a point where we admit to ourselves that we need some help. We're exhausted. We're not having nearly as much fun as we thought we would. In fact, all the things we do to try to ease the burden of being kings and queens seem to make things worse. The toys we never have enough time to play with. The casual drink every evening that grows into a habit and then becomes a source of tension with those who love us. The flirtatious banter with a coworker that starts innocently enough but becomes more and more of a distraction and then a cause for dissatisfaction and temptation. Life in the Kingdom of Me just isn't going the way we thought it would, and that's when we begin to think about God. Maybe if we could get closer to God it would help us run our kingdoms better, and life would be the way it was supposed to be. And here's how the journey typically unfolds.

First, a realization: eventually we will die and our kingdoms will end, and we hope God can help us with that little problem. Or maybe we reach out because we lost our job or our marriage is suffering or we have a chronic illness, and we realize that the resources of our kingdoms are insufficient for the demands of life. So we look beyond ourselves and beyond others. And we reach out to God.

Believe it or not, that's all God needs to move. He has always been there, working to draw us to Him. He has been actively wooing us back home, even as we tried to build our own kingdoms. He wants us. He wants *all* of us. He is not in heaven looking down on us in anger, ready to teach us our lessons. He is waiting to help us. He's eager for a relationship with us, even if we're immature and really still pretty self-centered.

As we reach out to God, He introduces us to His Son, Jesus. For many of us, that help feels more personal and more practical: if we accept Jesus, we won't go to hell. And who wants to go to hell? Further, Jesus became a person; He died for us. He's not a far-away deity but a more intimate friend. And this is a good thing.

Unfortunately, some of us view "accepting Jesus" simply as a "get out of hell" card. We of course are relieved that the life-after-death problem is figured out, and we really feel better about life knowing that we're not alone, because God is there to help us with our lives. As we continue on this journey, things improve in our lives. We really *do* have more peace and joy. God helps us with the assorted problems that show up in everyday life. The more we let God into our kingdoms, the better things are. And that's the problem.

We might not put it this crassly, but we view God as Someone who can assist us with *our* lives. We're still in our kingdoms, and because we were never designed to be kings and queens, as long as we stay in our kingdoms we will never experience the best God has for us. At this point, our journey reaches a crossroads. And it's where many of us stall, wondering if this is how life is supposed to be. We've got a bit of God in our kingdoms and we sense that there is more, but we're afraid of what it will take to find it.

We've brought God into our kingdoms as a sort of high-level

advisor. But we are still the CEOs, the kings or queens. While God's advice is helpful, keeping Him in an advisory role is, ultimately, not going to get us what we want. It's not ever going to get us a life of more.

In order to experience the best God has for us, something has to die.

Losing Your Life to Gain It

I know that sounds weird and not very appealing. I've been hinting at a better *life*. Suggesting that there's a much better way for you to *live*. And now I bring death into the picture? What's *that* all about?

As I said, back in the beginning God and human beings lived in perfect intimacy. There was only one King. The only condition He placed on having that kind of intimate relationship was that we let Him be King. When we rebelled, we rejected God as King. In order for us to return to that kind of intimacy we must take off our little crowns, lay down our little scepters, and walk out the door of our little castles and into the kingdom of God. That is at once one of the scariest and most liberating things we can ever do.

Jesus said that to gain the life that is truly life we have to lose our lives (see Matthew 16:25). We have to open our hand and let go, and that can be hard.

Laying down our own crowns feels scary. It goes against every-thing we value and have been taught about self-sufficiency, about ambition, about the "right" way to live our lives. What we don't realize is how we've bought into the culture around us that is based on achieving and acquiring. We've been trained since childhood to be consumers, and we approach faith that way. As a result, many of us settle for consuming God. We might not call it that, but the truth is, we take a little of God here and a little of God there in order to make our lives better, and it works. But then we hear a still, small voice—maybe just a whisper at first—telling us that there's something wrong with living this way. We ignore it at first, but the voice gets louder, more difficult to ignore. We know what we need to do, but we're afraid. As hard as it is being a king or queen, at least we know what to expect. We have the illusion of control. We have no idea what will happen if we abdicate our thrones, so we hold on, content that at least we have fire insurance. We know we will eventually join God and live with Him in eternity. We have no idea what life would be like if we gave up control of our kingdoms, so we never risk it. We simply hold on.

Several years ago I heard the poet David Whyte quote the Taoist philosopher Wei Wu Wei, who said, "Why are you unhappy? Because 99.9 percent of everything you think, and of everything you do, is for yourself—and there isn't one." In the context of our faith, living solely for ourselves is futile. It will always disappoint because that isn't the way God designed us. We cling to our kingdoms because we think we have so much that we are reigning and ruling over. We think we have very large kingdoms with tons of valuable assets and things of lasting value. But the reality is, everything in our kingdoms will one day be gone. In this present life all of it feels very real and very urgent, and it feels like if we didn't have it something in us would die. But our kingdoms are illusions, mirages. They don't exist. Oddly enough, to gain what will last, we have to let go.

Jesus said over and over that He had to die for something new to be born. He had to abdicate His throne for a season, and actually become a servant, in order for us to be restored to the one true King. Something must die so that something new may be born. What must really die is our kingdom. Our kingdoms are bankrupt; they're in foreclosure and there is no value to the assets. I'm sorry to be the one to have to tell you that, but it's true.

The idea of walking away from our own kingdoms makes us feel anxious and afraid. We have so much invested in them, and the idea of one day abandoning them completely, not even putting up a For Sale sign, is terrifying. But if you desire everything God has for you, that's exactly what has to happen. What you come to realize is that your kingdom actually has no value in God's economy. The only truly good and lasting things are the things of God, not the things of us.

How do we access the things of God? How do we live the life that is truly life, the life of more that God intended in creation and that Jesus offers us through redemption? What in our thinking and in our faith practice needs to change so that we can live a life of more? That is what the rest of this book will explore.

REFLECT

> Then the LORD God formed the man from the dust
> of the ground. He breathed the *breath of life* into the
> man's nostrils, and the man became a *living person.*
> (Genesis 2:7, NLT)

What is appealing to you about being the king or queen of your
own kingdom? Be honest; it's okay. What's the downside?

PART 2

n part 2, we're turning a corner. We're going to get very practical. The rest of this book will talk about how to live a life of more, the abundant life that Jesus promised us. I'm going to share what we learned from talking to real people who actually live this way. We're going to dig beyond the numbers in our data. After studying half a million church attendees, we found a small group who live with more peace, joy, satisfaction, and contentment. How did they get there? How do they live? What choices do they make that move them forward on a journey toward a life that is different from most people's?

When we studied the data and talked with these people, patterns emerged. While each story was unique, we found similar threads woven through all their stories. The threads fit into two categories: shifts in thinking and shifts in action. And it appeared that those two shifts had a symbiotic relationship: thinking and actions reinforced one another, and together, moved people toward greater intimacy with God.

You might have heard the term *paradigm shift*. Your paradigm is simply your framework for understanding how some aspect of life works. When your paradigm shifts, you suddenly see things differently, which opens up new possibilities, higher creativity, and a completely

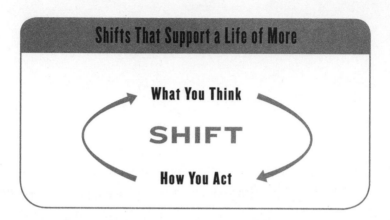

different perspective. A life of more depends on several key shifts in your thinking and actions.

Each of the following chapters will offer one shift in thinking and one simple action—one practical way that you can create some space in your life to experience intimacy with God, to connect with Him and let go of your own kingdom. These shifts will move you toward a life of more. And these shifts are never fully completed; you can't just check them off your list. Rather, you go deeper into each of them. You find there is always more to discover.

By the way, you don't have to do anything perfectly, because you can't. The whole journey is bathed in grace. These shifts will help you begin to experience God in a new way. We'll unpack what it means to live a life of more, one change at a time.

One more thing. At the conclusions of chapters 5 through 10, in addition to "Reflect" there will also be "Remember," a brief thought designed to summarize the heart of each chapter so we don't forget.

CHAPTER 5

From Inside
to Outside

When I was growing up, I remember feeling excited any time my parents bought a new appliance for our house. A new washer or dryer was great, a new refrigerator even better! Why? Not because I was thrilled about clean clothes or cold food. What interested me was the fact that these large appliances were delivered in huge cardboard boxes.

To a couple of little boys, that giant cardboard box was not just a box. With a little imagination, it became a fort, a castle, a cabin, even a boat. Whenever we would get ahold of a large box, my brother and I would decorate it inside and out, throw some blankets inside, stash some snacks or toys in there, and make it ours. We imagined it to be all sorts of things, but we knew this: it was ours.

Our parents sometimes even let us sleep in the box in the backyard. Of course, we knew that the box was just temporary and didn't really provide much protection at all, especially against the rain. In fact, in the heat of a Texas summer, being inside a box was incredibly uncomfortable. We didn't care. We enjoyed having our own secret place, our own little world. Eventually, we grew tired of our box fort. It was fun for a while, but we really didn't want to live in a box all the time.

Do You Live in a Box?

Many of us live in a box. It's the small box known as the Kingdom of Me. We control what happens there. We occasionally might feel a bit cramped, but we really like being in charge.

The Kingdom of Me box is safe and secure. It gives us protection, or at least the illusion of it, and a place to manage and control. We tell ourselves everything is going to be just fine as long as we can stay in the box.

Which would be great, except that it's a lie. Ultimately, life is not found inside a box. And because Jesus wants us to live life to the full—a life of more—He calls us to come out of the box. Much like He called Lazarus out of the grave, Jesus calls to us, "Come out! Open up your box, walk out, and find your life" (see John 11:43). There is no life inside the box. There is no life inside the Kingdom of Me, and we have to come out, into God's kingdom.

In my own life, I had to come to a point where I made a fundamental shift. Instead of asking God to help me with my life, I had to die to my own life and begin living God's life. I had to find my way out of the Kingdom of Me.

I had to ask myself: Where do I want to live? Do I want to live inside the box where I continue living in my own kingdom, consuming God as I see fit, asking Him to help me with my life as I continue to work really hard to handle my kingly responsibilities of protecting and providing for my life?

Jesus said, "Whoever finds their life will lose it, and whoever loses their life for my sake will find it" (Matthew 10:39). Leaving the box is losing your life for Jesus's sake, and it is the only way to find real life.

As we said in the previous chapter, sometimes we try to add a bit of God to our lives, to our kingdoms. We want to bring God into our box, have Him help us fix it up. But ultimately, that doesn't really change us in the way we'd hoped. It doesn't satisfy us.

In order to live the life we really want, we have to shift our thinking: from Inside to Outside. We must make the courageous decision to get out of our boxes, leave our own kingdoms, and allow ourselves to be consumed by Love Himself. We declare there is only one God, one King, and it is not us or anyone else walking on the planet.

When we leave our kingdoms, we are really returning home. We're finally going back to the way it was supposed to be. This is the path to find the "more out of life" that we have always wanted but couldn't quite seem to get. This is the abundant life Jesus said He came to give us. This is what we were made for, this intimate relationship with the King. All sources of anxiety and worry are gone because now we don't have to provide and protect our kingdoms. God has everything we need. He *is* everything we need.

Jesus Himself left His "box" by coming to earth. He let go of His throne in heaven to come, not as a wealthy or powerful king, but as a baby in a poor family in a small town. He definitely got out of His box, and He invites us to do the same, because the whole world is waiting for you when you leave the box. But more importantly, God is with you when you get out of your box.

The Gift of Freedom

We tend to think that a gift comes in a box. But in this case, the gift is outside the box. The gift is the freedom that comes from trusting God enough to get out of the box of our own kingdoms and live in the wide-open space of God's kingdom.

While it is scary to leave the box of our own kingdoms, it's important to realize that we're actually not as safe as we think in the box. In fact, all our striving to provide and protect is really motivated by fear. In the Kingdom of Me, fear rules the day. We're constantly worried about losing what we've worked so hard to acquire, whether it is money, power, relationships, or control.

This process in my own life didn't happen overnight, but it did begin with an essential shift in my thinking (and thus, my behavior). I began to think deeply about Jesus's first request in the Lord's Prayer: "Your kingdom come . . . on earth as it is in heaven." I've probably recited that over a thousand times, but it was only after I left my own kingdom that it made sense to me. Until that point I thought those words were really saying, "Jesus, please come physically, right now. Come back and rule and reign on this earth like it says in Revelation, putting an end to all this pain, hunger, and violence in the world."

When I left my own kingdom, I realized that praying "Your kingdom come" means asking that God's kingdom would come into my life and other people's lives—not someday, but now. That is what Jesus was saying. He was not asking the Father to bring all this to an end now. He was praying that we would embrace His kingdom in the here and now. That we would experience the freedom He brings, not someday in heaven, but right now.

Praying "Your will be done" means you are willing to abandon your own kingdom so there will be only one kingdom under one King and that King's will would be done on earth (in your life) as it is in heaven. In other words, this oft-repeated prayer means that God's will—His desire for the world—can be accomplished every day right here on earth when we leave our kingdoms. Instead of consuming God, we are consumed by Him, overwhelmed by His love, His goodness, His power. We are so consumed by Him that His thoughts are our thoughts and He is able to demonstrate His love for others through us.

Where are you living right now? Inside or outside the box? In your kingdom, with a bit of God brought in when you need Him, or in God's kingdom? Answering this question, and changing your answer to it, takes time. Little by little, you can live more and more outside the box if you're willing to simply ask yourself each day, *Where am I now? Am I inside the box or outside the box?* And then be brave enough, with God's help, to step outside the box each day, each hour, and trust God to show you how to live in His kingdom. To confess to Him the times you're trying to run the kingdom, and to start again.

I've done my share of planning and hard work and ended up with a kingdom filled with stuff that had no value. And I work for a church! We must die to the idea that we are in charge. That we have power. That we can build kingdoms better than God's. If we truly desire life as it was supposed to be lived, we must abdicate the thrones of our own lives and submit to the one true King.

Submission. Yeah, that word means it won't be easy. When I decided I had had enough of being my own king and walked out of my castle, I did so with great resolve and sincerity. I was done with being king. And then a few days later I walked up to my old castle, opened the doors, and walked right back in. I stayed for a few days before I was reminded of how much I didn't like being king, and I left my castle (again) for God's kingdom. That pattern repeated itself over and over in different areas of my life where I was still holding on to a piece of my own little kingdom. But that's okay. God helps us as we vacillate between our little kingdoms and His grand one. He's tender and patient and kind, and that always makes us want to stay in His kingdom longer. Each time, we let go of a bit of our kingdoms and see more clearly how much better God's kingdom is. Eventually, your own little kingdom becomes a faint memory, with little to pull you back.

While this shift out of the box didn't happen all at once for me, a key turning point happened when I got a call from my doctor.

THE PHONE CALL

In September of 2004, at my annual physical, I felt healthy but mentioned to my doctor that I'd had some pain on my left side, in my stomach, and more recently in my lower back. I assumed it was not a big deal. I figured the discomfort in my stomach was simply stress.

Just the week before, my wife had been playing with our children and had broken her ankle (she was trying to demonstrate a cool karate move—don't ask!). So I spent the month of August doing back-to-school things with our three children. It was kind of chaotic with Lynn not being able to walk or drive for about a month. At the same time, at work we were a few months away from opening a new seven-thousand-seat auditorium, and there were a lot of last-minute details to tend to. Pressure at work was high; I was needed at home; my wife was sidelined. I felt stretched thin.

My doctor said all looked good and the pain I was feeling was probably just stress related, but to be safe he ordered a colonoscopy and a CAT scan of my abdomen. While that was a bit unusual for someone my age, just forty-two, I figured it would be good to rule out any problems.

The colonoscopy, while not the most pleasant thing to prepare for, went fine—no issues. But it was the phone call I received from my doctor following the CAT scan that I will never forget. He told me things looked fine in my stomach region, but there was this cyst on my left kidney. He said it was two or three centimeters in diameter and was probably not a big deal, but I should meet with a urologist he knew to make sure. The word *cyst* didn't seem too scary. I thought cysts were common, and after doing some Internet research later that day, I found that was indeed the case.

A few weeks later at my urology appointment, the doctor placed the CAT scan films up on a light board and started walking me through the pictures showing slice after slice of my midsection.

"Here is the bottom of your kidney," he said as a small portion emerged on the screen. He continued, moving slowly from the bottom to the top. As he worked his way up, a dark spot emerged on the screen. "Here is where the cyst starts, on the left side." It grew bigger and bigger, and eventually, the spot looked bigger than my kidney itself. At that point I felt a wave of panic. Seeing that dark mass and realizing it was inside of me actually made me sick to my stomach. Despite the doctor's description of its size, a cyst in my mind was something the size of a raisin, or maybe a marble. But this thing looked to be the size of a billiard ball. "It might be benign," the doctor said, "but its strange shape raises the real possibility that it's malignant." We talked about the various options. I tried to focus and act calm. But I felt dizzy, nauseous. And scared.

My urologist wanted to remove my entire left kidney. He thought that would be the easiest way to go about it. He said another option was to remove the tumor (funny how fast it went from a cyst to a tumor) but not the kidney. But when he said that, the look on his face changed. "But that's an awful surgery and a very, very painful recovery," he said. He suggested that because I was young and healthy, I should let him remove one kidney. A person can function with one, and it was a much less invasive surgery.

I told him I would think it over and probably seek a second opinion.

I left the office, took the elevator down to the parking garage, got into my car, and just lost it. Tears filled my eyes. This could not be happening. It was like a bad dream. I had three young children ages eight, six, and two. Cancer. I came to the appointment thinking it was not a big deal, and I left wondering how long I had to live. I called Lynn and told her everything. She listened sympathetically and then with great calm said, "We need to go to the Mayo Clinic. I will call them now." We hung up and I started the thirty-five-minute drive back to my office. Within fifteen minutes my phone rang. It was Lynn. "You have an appointment at Mayo in three weeks with an expert on what you have."

Three weeks later, at the Mayo Clinic in Rochester, Minnesota, we met an extraordinary urologist, Dr. Matt Gettman. He took one look at my CAT scan and said without hesitation, "That thing needs to come out." I mentioned how the doctor in Chicago wanted to take out my entire left kidney, and he turned, looked me square in the eye, and said, "Oh no, we're not going to take out your kidney. You need your kidneys. We can get rid of this thing without taking out your entire kidney." But then he said, "Greg, it's an awful surgery. I'll need to cut you from your belly button all the way around to the middle of the left side of your back. And the recovery is one of the most painful of any surgical procedures."

So we left his office and scheduled the surgery for the next month, before Thanksgiving. The surgery was successful. Dr. Gettman was able to remove the cyst and all cancerous tissue, while leaving me with 90 percent of my left kidney fully functioning. I remember when I came out of anesthesia later that day, I didn't feel much pain at all. It was not as painful as the two doctors said it would be. Then the next morning, still not much pain. I remember being on the phone, talking to friends and family members. Easy.

I didn't feel much pain because they had given me a spinal block during surgery that stopped all nerve traffic from my waist down. When it wore off later that day, it was like getting hit by a truck. A very large truck that was not braking at all upon impact. That pain stayed with me for weeks, despite morphine and other exotic and not-so-exotic pain medicines.

After eight days in the hospital, we drove the 330 miles back to our home. It was two days before Thanksgiving, with Christmas just around the corner. I had already planned to be home from work until the first week of January, thinking that would be more than enough time to recover. I was very, very wrong.

All the muscles in my core, and the nerves associated with those muscles, had been severed and needed to heal. I really could not move. I was taking a tremendous amount of pain medicine just in order to exist.

Prior to this surgery, I'd had other medical experiences. Healing from illness was simple. After I got enough rest and took the medicine I was supposed to take, I would wake up each morning feeling slightly better. Even if it took me a week or maybe two weeks, I knew I was getting better, because I could feel the improvement every day.

But this recovery was very different. Day after day after day I woke up and felt no better. Day after day I noticed no incremental improvement. Weeks into the recovery (or hoped-for recovery), it dawned on me that I had no idea when, or even if, I was going to feel better.

Then reality crystalized in a powerful idea that rocked me: I couldn't do *anything*. I couldn't do my work. I tried e-mailing back and forth with colleagues, but I realized I couldn't add value because I wasn't there and I wasn't thinking clearly because I was on so much pain medicine. At the same time I'd see my wife with three small children, getting ready for Christmas and everything that involved, and I couldn't help at all. I couldn't drive, I couldn't be out, and I couldn't walk very well.

I couldn't play with my children; I couldn't do anything they needed. They saw me being so sick and weak, and I hated the thought of them looking at me like that and wondering if I was going to be okay.

I became very depressed when I realized that I couldn't do anything. I couldn't make myself better; I couldn't provide for my family. Thankfully, I was still being paid, but I realized that I couldn't do anything that generated affirmation and a sense of self-worth. And it hit me: I'd been living on affirmation for forty years.

Accomplishment, and the affirmation that came with it, was like oxygen to me. I couldn't get the affirmation from work that I've done a good job and I'm a good person. I couldn't get the affirmation from my wife that I was helping out at home. I couldn't help with my kids. I couldn't do anything in life that added value. I couldn't provide for my family, I couldn't protect my family, I couldn't do anything.

I got to the end of myself in that moment and realized that my life was built around this identity that I could *do* things, that I was competent. I had built a fairly sizable Kingdom of Me, not from a monetary point of view, but from a sense of achievement and worth and value and a self-perception that I could do things.

I had been the master of my own kingdom. And in that season of physical and emotional pain, when all my accomplishments were stripped away, I saw the charade of it all. It was almost pathetic because I was so sure that I was all-powerful, all-competent. I was completely undone. I actually had moments when I thought my life was not worth living. I would ask myself, *Why do I keep going? What's the point? I have nothing of value to offer my family, my work.* I couldn't do anything. It was an awful, miserable feeling.

The thing that saved my life, literally, was a book my colleague Mike Breaux gave me the day before I left for the hospital. It was a devotional titled *Who I Am in Christ* by Neil Anderson. Anderson's other books are about spiritual warfare, with titles like *Victory Over the Darkness* and *The Bondage Breaker,* so I kind of wondered why Mike chose to give me that book at that time. I set it aside. About three weeks into my recovery I picked up the book. It contained thirty-six short chapters and meditations with scripture. The chapter titles included "I Am God's Child," "I Am Secure," "I Am Assured That All Things Work Together for Good," "I Am Significant," "I Can Do All Things Through Christ Who Strengthens Me." The book, which reminded me of these truths about my identity in Christ, also reminded me that apart from Him I am nothing. But with Him I am everything.

That book came into the crucible of pain I was in and began to change and refine me. I confessed to God that I had built an idol out of my life, that apart from Him I could do nothing. That was a moment of full surrender that I'll never forget because I realized that God loved me anyway. I was His beloved child. In that moment, I came out of the box in the most profound way.

SURRENDER TO LOVE

Once you've left the box, you need somewhere to go. But where? On a practical level, leaving the box means living in God's kingdom, which means surrendering your life, little by little. The Bible talks about God becoming greater and our own needs and agendas becoming less and less important. That's the process you engage in when you leave the box.

Sometimes we think about surrender as defeat, where we're crushed by a more powerful force. Because of that, we often live in fear and resist surrender.

Fear is driven, ironically, by self-reliance. If I'm feeling afraid, it means I still want to be in control. I feel anxiety and fear that I'm not in control. But the antidote to fear is faith. And faith means being fully grounded in reality: the reality that I cannot control or move or influence anything in any meaningful way. So my fear of losing control is overcome by letting go of control, which feels counterintuitive. But that's the reality in God's kingdom, where you gain your life by losing it, where you go down to go up.

This is God's created world. *His* world. His kingdom is the only real kingdom. He is King. Now here is the kicker. Do I believe I am a treasured child of the King? If I believe that, I have nothing to fear. I can surrender, not in defeat, but in faith.

In God's kingdom, surrender feels more like falling in love. We surrender to love, which is exhilarating and risky but ultimately the only way we're going to experience joy. We let go, believing that God will take care of us. We trust.

Imagine if I came home from work one night and opened the garage door to find my three children rummaging through the garbage cans in the garage. My oldest son with an empty pizza box in one hand, my daughter digging through vegetable peelings, handing the occasional apple core to my youngest son. Imagine me asking, "What on earth are you doing? Why are you looking for food in the garbage can?"

And imagine if my three children looked at me and said, "Well, we weren't sure you were going to come home and feed us tonight, so we decided we'd better fend for ourselves." You may think, *Well, that's crazy. You feed your kids every day; there's a kitchen full of food in your house.*

When we choose not to trust God, we go garbage picking to try to feed ourselves. We forget, or don't trust, that in God's kingdom there is plenty. We are like children digging in a garbage can when there is more than enough provision in our Father's house.

As a dad, if I saw my children foraging for food in a garbage can, I wouldn't say they were bad. I'd say, "Don't you know that I love you and I will take care of you?" I would feel overwhelmed with love, with a desire to give them good things, and maybe sad that they didn't believe I'd feed them when I'd done that their whole lives. But I would reach toward them in love, toss the empty boxes and apple cores in the trash, and say, "Come on into the kitchen and let me make you something fresh, nourishing, and delicious, because I love you and it delights me to provide for you. You can trust me."

God is a Father like that. When we let fear erode our trust and start foraging for ourselves instead of enjoying His provision, He doesn't shame us. He calls us, with love and tenderness, back out of our little kingdoms and into His kingdom, where there is always plenty. He invites us to the table. All He asks us to give up, or surrender, is digging through the trash.

In surrender, we let go of our own agendas, our own lives. It's not so that we can do tasks for God (although that might eventually happen). It's so that we can have more of God. We can experience Him more fully; we can live in His love, surrender to that love, and just let it fill us and fulfill us. It's so we can eat our fill at His table—even though we have to trust that He'll provide all we need.

In that daily surrender, we move from wanting our own life, to wanting God's life for us, to simply wanting God. Because we realize if we have God, we have everything we need. We realize that Jesus was right: when we seek God's kingdom first, all these other things that matter will be added to us. The first thing is to seek after God Himself and want Him more than anything else.

Each time you return home to God's kingdom, you will realize that you don't have to crawl in through the back door. You don't have to be ashamed or embarrassed, because you are a child of the King! You begin to embrace the truths that I found in that little devotional my friend gave me while I was recovering from surgery: "You're loved." "You are secure." "You are significant." "God is working for good in your life."

You serve a King who knows you better than you know yourself and loves you regardless of anything you've done. Each day you spend in His kingdom, that glorious truth sinks in deeper to the very depths of your being. Being loved in this way makes returning to your own kingdom, your old box, less and less appealing. When you were king, you were a pretender. Now you are royalty. You begin to live the life that is truly life, the life that Jesus offers—a life that is the way it was supposed to be from the very beginning.

God really does want to help you. He's not angry with you. He loves you. Through His Son, Jesus, you have been given the gift of a new life, one that is free of guilt and shame. Because of your relationship with Him through Jesus, He's your friend, an ever-present companion to guide and help you. He is the best friend you could ever imagine, always there for you, always able to drop whatever He's doing to come help you do anything. But in reality, He is more than a friend. He is the King. And to enjoy the life you truly desire—the way it was always supposed to be—you have to transcend the idea of Jesus just as your friend so you can see Jesus as your King and Ruler of the one true kingdom.

Jesus invites us into friendship, but eventually we make another shift: He's not only our best friend; He is our trusted leader and authority. The relationship goes deeper, and trust grows stronger.

It's very soft, and it's very subtle, that decision where we shift from having God as our friend to having Him as our King. It's a quiet but profound decision that happens in a deep part of our souls where we call out and say, "Yes, I was made to be under someone's authority—someone I can trust completely. I was made to be with my Creator in deep intimacy."

I was driving to work one morning, listening to a new worship CD from Gateway Church. The last song on the disc is called "The Whole Earth," and it is about God's kingdom coming and about Jesus being holy—the perfect, awe-inspiring, majestic King. I sang along with a cup of Starbucks green tea in one hand. As I turned a corner I saw a little girl standing on the sidewalk. She looked about six years old, and she'd stopped for a moment to zip up her coat. Once that was done she took off running with that joyful exuberance children have, sprinting to her bus stop at the end of the street. For whatever reason, watching that little girl with so much life and energy, I just started crying. Tears fell down my face, and eventually I had to pull over as the song continued: "Holy, Holy is the Lord Almighty."

As I sat in the parking lot listening to the song and thinking about that little girl, I wondered why I was having such a reaction. I'd had a good night's sleep. I was in a good mood. I wasn't feeling overly emotional about anything at that moment. And yet something overwhelmed me. I asked God to show me what He was trying to say to me.

Then it all came together. I was on my way to work to lead a meeting about our Christmas program. The image of Jesus coming as a baby, and then eventually reigning as King, swept over me in a powerful new way. God knew we would be terrified to embrace Him as King—as "holy and almighty." He knows us so well, and He knew we wouldn't want to submit to a King—that we would want to be our own kings. So He came as a baby, to a poor family in an obscure village. He came in a completely unintimidating, humble, quiet way. Only God could come up with that. To bring us back home, to win us over, He sent a baby. Isn't that just the kind of King you want?

SHIFT IN ACTION

In order to live outside the box, we must decide daily to do so. We must decide to live in God's kingdom.

How do we get there? What shift in action will keep us from running back to our own kingdoms? It's simple but difficult: we must learn to say we're sorry.

According to our research, one of the core actions that strengthens this daily decision and builds deep intimacy with God is the simple action of saying to God, "I'm sorry," when we make choices that hurt other people or hurt God Himself.

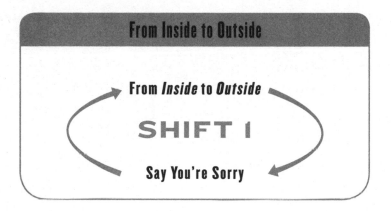

Saying you're sorry is sometimes called confession. Perhaps you grew up in a religious tradition that demanded confession or laid on guilt for mistakes you had made, and the idea of confession is laden with lots of negative thoughts. But I'm not talking about that. Confession is simply saying "I'm sorry" to God when we hurt people He created and loves or, more likely, when we do things that demonstrate our lack of trust and belief that He is good and that He loves us.

When we worry, we are telling God, "I don't trust You. I don't think You can help, and more importantly, I don't think You *want* to help." We start digging through garbage cans, thinking we have to fend for ourselves. That's hardly a path to intimacy. In fact, it's a path straight back into the box. The doorway out of the Kingdom of Me, into God's kingdom, is saying you're sorry.

When we honestly confess that we're not trusting God or that we went our own way instead of His, intimacy is restored. In that moment of honesty you will sense Jesus saying, *I forgive you.* Because He always does, regardless of how many times you have to ask Him to forgive you. If you do something you know is wrong or something you know is based in fear or worry, stop right then and there and confess it. He won't shame you. He's not angry. He knows it's because you're afraid, and He wants to reassure you. It's part of the deal we get with full intimacy. You don't have to be ashamed. You don't have to hide. He knows what you did before you tell Him, but He wants you to trust Him enough, wants you to believe He's really got your back, so that you never think of hiding *anything* from Him. Isn't that a much better way to live?

You may also need to read over and over again this incredible description of the way it is supposed to be between you and God:

> For I am convinced that neither death nor life, neither
> angels nor demons, neither the present nor the future, nor
> any powers, neither height nor depth, nor anything else
> in all creation, will be able to separate us from the love of
> God that is in Christ Jesus our Lord. (Romans 8:38–39)

We have been so conditioned to thinking God is "out there" and we have to work really hard to find Him that we've missed the whole point of why He created us in the first place: He wants to have a deep, personal, intimate relationship with you. Nothing in all of creation can separate you from God. If you're new at this, your reflexive thought might be, *I've really blown it this time. There's no way God is going to forgive this one.* Not to get spooky on you, but I believe that's the Enemy—the forces of evil—trying to interfere with your intimate relationship with God. And the Enemy always uses the same thing to defeat you: a lie. This is why you need to go back regularly and hear those words of truth: nothing in all of creation can separate you from God.

Saying we're sorry to God who loves us unconditionally is freeing. It's simply taking a look at how we've lived, the choices we've made, honestly and prayerfully. We ask God to show us the areas where we are still trying to live as kings and queens and then confess those to God. We ask Him to give us clarity on ways we are not trusting Him, and we choose to trust again. Confession is not about shame but about restoring intimacy.

You may ask, "If God knows what I've done, why do I have to confess it?" A couple of thoughts here: God knows what you've done, but do you? Really? We tend to brush our mistakes under the rug; we tend not to notice the ways in which we've walked back into our castle in the Kingdom of Me. We tend to rationalize our sin, make excuses, or minimize. We tend to call our worry and fear "being responsible." When we behave selfishly, by definition we're unaware of it because we're focused on ourselves. Taking time for a bit of self-examination and honest conversation with God helps us see the ways in which we're living in the box. By naming our mistakes or our lack of trust and saying we're sorry, we get clarity on what needs to change. We get our bearings, so to speak. The action reinforces the change in our thinking. If we want to go somewhere, we have to know where we're starting. Regular confession is like checking our GPS, seeing where we've gotten off track. It's like turning the car around and acknowledging our mistakes enough to change direction.

If you're a parent or if you observe small children, you're usually aware when they did something wrong. They broke something, hit someone, didn't share their toys. And yet we teach children to admit their mistakes, to specifically name them, and to say, "I'm sorry." Sometimes they don't say it enthusiastically, but we teach them to say they're sorry because it will help them form good character.

As a dad, some of my most endearing moments with my kids happened when they would come to me and say, "Daddy, I'm sorry." They'd admit to something they'd done wrong. Nine times out of ten, I already knew what they'd done. But having them say it and apologize made my heart swell with love. God is our heavenly Father. Even if He already knows what we did to mess up, He feels nothing but love when we come to Him and say we're sorry. He extends grace to us and welcomes us back into the unhindered intimacy that we were made for.

Saying you're sorry builds trust through conversation in which you might say something like this: *God, I confess that I have tried to build my own kingdom, even with Your help, believing that I could protect and provide for my life. I declare to You that there is only one God and it's not me; there is only one King and it's not me. That You, O God, are the one true God, that Your Son, Jesus, is the one true King, and that through Your Spirit You are everywhere and in everything. I trust You.*

REFLECT

> And now we live in fellowship with the true God
> because we live in fellowship with his Son, Jesus
> Christ. He is the only true God, and he is eternal
> *life.* (1 John 5:20, NLT)

Where are you living right now—inside or outside the box? Do you find it hard or easy to say, "I'm sorry"?

Bonus: Go buy a small box. I got a cardboard one at a local craft store, about three inches square. Size and shape don't matter. Put it in a place where you will see it every day. I have mine on my desk. When you see it, ask yourself the question, "Where am I living right now?" If you answer, "Inside the box," reflect on why you have sought the shelter of "the cardboard." Maybe you need to say you're sorry.

REMEMBER

Each day, begin by deciding where you want to live: inside the box where you are king or queen, or outside the box where God has everything waiting for you. Throughout each day, if you sense part of you has retreated into the box, simply tell God, "I'm sorry," and head back out into the light.

From Me
to We

So let's say you decide to go ahead and leave your own kingdom and exit your box, even if only for a few minutes. The first steps "outside" can be scary. Outside is a very big place, with no perceivable walls or limits. You can feel unprotected at first and wonder how God expects you to live in this crazy space. Remember, you are used to providing for and protecting yourself. This feels chaotic and unpredictable. And so you call out to God, wanting Him to come be with you, wondering where He is.

Chances are God is not exactly where you think He is.

When I was a kid, I imagined God up in heaven. I remember lying in my bed when all was quiet in the house and I would pray to God up there in heaven. I remember imagining my prayers flying up through the roof of the house and in some magic way He heard them even though He was way far off in heaven and I was in my little bed in Port Arthur, Texas. That's where God was to me—somewhere far, far away. But He could still hear me. The idea of a God who could hear (and would listen!) from so far away somehow comforted my little eight-year-old heart.

Later in life I learned that God came down to earth in the person of Jesus and that He walked among us. I thought that was fantastic.

God wasn't so far away after all. He was right here on planet Earth. And then I heard something that transformed my life: I could have a relationship with Him; He actually cared about me and was someone I could talk to like I talked to friends. In my twenties, I would drive in my car and imagine Him in the seat next to me, and I would talk to Him. Sometimes I would imagine Him in my apartment sitting in an empty chair across from me and I would just chat with God. Pretty cool, I thought.

It was around this time I first read the classic (and overquoted) poem "Footprints in the Sand" by Mary Stevenson. I loved the image of the single set of footprints made by God as He carries us along the beach in the tough times of life. I was comforted by that beautiful image—God picking me up and holding me when life was too difficult to handle. I loved to think of God being so close that He knew when I needed Him and would rush to me and carry me through the hard times.

Carrie Underwood's hit song "Jesus, Take the Wheel" expresses a similar view of God. I'm sure you've heard the song about a girl driving home for Christmas, "low on faith and gasoline," feeling some regret about the road she's chosen in life. When the car hits a patch of ice, she throws up her hands in desperation and prays for Jesus to take the wheel, admitting she can't steer on black ice and also that she can't manage her own life very well and needs help.

The song and the poem may be a bit sentimental, but they offer a comforting image of Jesus who shows up just when we need Him. What a difference from my childhood view of God being way up there in heaven. As I grew in my faith, it seemed that God kept getting closer and closer to me. Now I understand Him to be right there next to me. We talk about Him being "closer than a brother" (Proverbs 18:24). Jesus promises, "I am with you always, to the very end of the age" (Matthew 28:20). And, "Where two or three gather together because they are mine, I will be right there among them" (Matthew 18:20, TLB).

It's comforting to know that God is always close by, ready to help when we need Him. It's an accurate picture of God. But it's not the complete picture.

WHERE IS THERE?

A lot of Christians talk about their relationship with God as a spiritual journey. A journey takes you from one place to another. You start here and go there. When I was a kid and we drove to visit relatives or take a vacation, those journeys were exciting because I always knew something fun and good was waiting for me. Even if we were delayed by traffic or had a flat tire, it didn't matter because I knew eventually we would arrive at our destination.

The notion of a journey also carries with it a sense of challenge or adventure. I think of those brave souls who climb Mount Everest and ordinary people who run marathons. Talk about difficult journeys. But the goal drives them—to get to the top of the world's highest mountain or just stagger across the finish line after running 26 miles and 385 yards. Every journey begins with a goal in mind. It's like the mythical pirate map with an *X* marking the spot where the treasure is hidden. Or like the *Lord of the Rings* trilogy where Frodo Baggins embarks on a quest to destroy the Ring. When I pack my own children in the car and hit the interstate, I know exactly where I'm going—from here to there. I know where there is.

So if we apply this image of a journey to our relationship with God—when we talk about our spiritual journeys—where is *there*? Where is it that we are going on this spiritual journey? What do we hope to accomplish? What challenges are we overcoming?

I used to think the destination of our spiritual journeys was God—that we're on this quest to know God better, to get closer to Him. That if we keep traveling down the spiritual highway, we'll finally run into God. But then one day I realized that the whole idea of God being "out there" is not only wrong, but it keeps us from experiencing the best God wants for us: full intimacy with Him. "Out there" implies that God is way off somewhere in His kingdom and I'm in mine. When I need help I can call out to Him and He comes to help me (see Psalm 34:17), and that's good. He has promised to hear us when we cry for help, and God never breaks His promises. But as much as He wants to help us when we need Him, He wants to be with us when things are going well too. God wants to have the most intimate relationship possible with us, just as He designed it in the beginning. I don't need to spend my life moving toward a "someday" because I can experience that intimacy right now.

God is not out there; He is here, and He is everything, fully present in your life. I said earlier that it seemed God kept getting closer to me as I grew in my understanding and faith. But the real growth occurred when I realized that in reality I was just getting better at seeing God, who had always been right there with me.

He is not driving the car; He's in you as you drive the car. He's not walking alongside you or even carrying you; He's in you as you walk. Wherever you go. When you think of Him as a "help desk" or a destination on your journey, it's because you are still living in your kingdom. But when you leave your kingdom, or get outside the box, as we talked about in the previous chapter, you're affirming this truth and saying to God, *I don't just need You when I'm having a difficult time. I don't need You only when I have that job interview or when I'm waiting for the results of my medical test. I don't just need You right now. I want You. I want to be with You always. 24/7.*

What's so much better about this picture of God is that we're not using Him, so to speak, but we're enjoying Him and His presence. It is our heart's true home—not to be close to God but to allow Him to live *in* us.

Outside of our own kingdoms, we move from consuming God to being fully consumed by Him. God is fully present in my life every moment. He cares about me personally, and He's not up in heaven like I imagined Him to be when I was eight years old. He's not even in the passenger seat. He is all around me *and* He is in me. He is in you. He's always been there.

When we think of God as far away or as someone we can conjure up to assist us when we're skidding out of control, we miss out on what God wants to give us. That is the heart of the problem: we really don't believe God wants us. We don't believe God simply desires intimacy with us. We figure He's got some hidden agenda, some demands He'll soon make.

The truth is, He's happy to carry you or take the wheel in a crisis, but more than that, God desires you—just you, in relationship with Him. That thought may make us uncomfortable. Our pride and our shame isolate us and shut us off from God. When we can overcome our pride (which tells us we can do it ourselves; we don't need anyone) and our shame (which tells us we can't do it; we're unworthy of help or love; no one would ever want us), we can understand that God wants us. He wants *all* of us.

SHIFT: FROM "ME" TO "WE"

In the previous chapter, we talked about the first of several shifts that people living in deep intimacy with God have made. We said that a life of more requires us to shift from living inside the box to outside the box, from living in the Kingdom of Me to living in God's kingdom. And we said the shift in action that goes with that and reinforces it is learning to say, "I'm sorry."

The next shift in thinking we need to make is from "me" to "we." What does that mean?

When you go through an average day, you probably find yourself thinking, *I've got to go here. I've got to do this. I've got to finish this project, run this errand, pick up the kids and the dry cleaning. I've got to get things done. I've got to think about what I'll do tomorrow.*

If you have a relationship with God or are trying to make God fit into your kingdom, you may even add, *I've got to read my Bible. I really should pray more. I ought to go to church. I've got to volunteer at Sunday school, and I've got to bake a cake for the potluck dinner.*

If you want to live a life of more, if you want to experience God in the way He meant for you to live, you have to make another fundamental shift. You must stop thinking "me" and start thinking "we." Remember, you have left your own kingdom (the Kingdom of Me) and have come into God's kingdom, where you are with the King 24/7.

Rather than thinking, *I've got to . . .* , begin to think, *We're going to . . .* you *and* God. Think of doing your day, moment by moment, with God. You're consumed by God and so everything you do is with Him—*God and I are doing this,* or *God and I are leading our small group,* or *We have a presentation for a client today*—because God is in you and with you not only at church or at work but at the gym, the grocery store, in every moment of every day.

Those who have made this shift or are in the process of making it think of everything in terms of "we." It begins with simply paying attention to your language, to the way that you talk to yourself.

So when you notice yourself saying or thinking "I" or "me," make a conscious shift and say or think "we." The change may feel awkward at first, but it's a habit that will bring you into a strong awareness of God's presence. By changing your words, you can change your thinking, which will change your attitudes, then your feelings, and finally your experiences. Shifting from "me" to "we" means you don't ask God to be with you in a particularly challenging situation you might face. Rather, you become aware that He's already there doing life with you. And you're aware of that so deeply that you begin to think "we" instead of "me." God is not assisting us. Rather, He's on point, leading the way, but with us and in us.

Jesus lived this way, modeling this in His relationship with the Father. And He taught it to His followers when He talked about "abiding" or staying in constant communion with God. He said, "Don't you believe that I am in the Father and the Father is in me? The words I speak are not my own, but my Father who lives in me does his work through me" (John 14:10, NLT). This is how He wants us to live as well.

However, despite God's passionate desire to know you intimately, He never forces Himself on anyone. When you insist on being the king or queen of your own little kingdom, He lets you keep Him out. When you need Him, He comes to your aid because He loves you. Most of us, as we get to know God, tend to have an "off and on" relationship with Him. When we first let Him in, we're excited and experience real fellowship with Him. The periods of closeness with God give us glimpses of what it could be like *all* the time, but once our needs are met, we go back to being king. It's all too easy to abandon "we" and slip back into thinking about "me." At least that's the way it was with me until I just got tired of being the king and realized I didn't have to work so hard to be close to God. Because He was closer than I thought.

God is *in* you.

Theologically, this reality is expressed in the Christian doctrine of the Trinity: God the Father, the Son, and the Holy Spirit. In one of His last discourses to His closest followers, Jesus promised, "I will ask the Father, and he will give you another advocate to help you and be with you forever" (John 14:16). That helper is the very Spirit of God, or Holy Spirit. Even in Old Testament times, before Jesus was sent to earth, there were certain prophets who were given the gift of the Holy Spirit, evidenced in full intimacy and a radical encounter with God. Now through Christ He gives every Christian the same opportunity for intimacy. We just need to change the way we think. Yes, God is in heaven, somewhere way out there that we cannot even comprehend, because He is everywhere. But He gives us His Spirit, who is capable of living in us.

At first, as I began to understand that I didn't have to try so hard to get close to God, I imagined Him inside of me. I thought of Him as an object about the size of my fist or a can of soup. I know that sounds really strange, but that's just how my mind works. I made the shift from the Kingdom of Me to the kingdom of God and thought of Him as being inside me almost like another organ. Yup, He's right there inside of me, next to my kidneys and liver and heart. It's a compelling image, but unfortunately it's faulty. He's not just another organ or a spirit camping out somewhere near my pancreas. He desires to fully dwell inside of me—to completely fill me so that I'm not just taking a little bit of God but am truly consumed with Him, so that I am one with Him and He fills every corner of my being. His thoughts are my thoughts, and His desires are mine. That's the picture we have to have in our minds if we desire true intimacy with God.

I love the way the apostle Paul wrote about this wonderful gift:

> I pray that out of his glorious riches he may strengthen you
> with power through his Spirit in your inner being, so that
> Christ may dwell in your hearts through faith. And I pray that
> you, being rooted and established in love, may have power,
> together with all the Lord's holy people, to grasp how wide
> and long and high and deep is the love of Christ, and to know
> this love that surpasses knowledge—that you may be filled to
> the measure of all the fullness of God. (Ephesians 3:16–19)

I'm always amazed when Christians who say they believe the Bible is absolutely true just sort of gloss over a passage like this: "You may be filled to the measure of all the fullness of God." Wow! Imagine that. "Filled to the measure" means *completely filled*. God's desire is to fill us to overflowing so that every pore of our being is permeated with His love. Could you imagine what the world would be like if every Christian truly believed this and allowed that love to take root inside of them so that all loved the world as God does?

THE BARRICADE WE BUILD

I'd like to tell you that I now live every day in full intimacy with God, but I don't. I can be blissfully enjoying His presence, allowing

His love to flow through me into the lives of others, when some bump in the road pushes me back into my own little kingdom.

But why? Why don't I let all of God's love and power inside of me? I know the best thing for me is to not have any barrier between me and God, to invite His full presence into my life. How can I do anything in life apart from Him? Jesus made this crystal clear. He said, "I am the vine; you are the branches. If you remain in me and I in you, you will bear much fruit; apart from me you can do nothing" (John 15:5). Nothing. Absolutely nothing of value or worth apart from Him. If I abide in Him and He in me, then a lot of good things will happen. If I don't, life is hard for me and those around me. It's that simple. So why do I go back to being my own king and keeping God distant when all He wants is to live fully in and through me?

It goes back to the kingdom thing. The barrier that I felt between God and me was not imposed on me but something that I built over time. I have sometimes said to God that there are still areas of my life where I just don't want Him to enter. So I built a barricade. I started rebuilding my box, my Kingdom of Me. Sometimes I'm not even aware of what I'm doing. But deep down, I don't want to relinquish control to God over that area of my life. I refuse to let Him in. The reason that I don't have more of God is because I've created a barrier. I let some of the walls of my kingdom stand. I've even barricaded or reinforced walls that I thought I'd dismantled.

Those walls must come down, but it may not happen all at once. I'd love to see them shattered forever but the truth is, it's a process. Some days you will live completely in God's kingdom, letting Him live inside of you. Some days you will discover a room in your castle that needs to be demolished. One simple way to take down the barricade is to be highly aware of the language and words you use in your self-talk and in talking to God. You need to practice saying "we" instead of "me." You also need to ignore the lies that the Enemy uses to keep us distant from God. Chief among them is the lie that says if God fully dwelt in you He would be disgusted at what He saw. That He would be revolted by you. That's just not true. It goes against God's very nature. God loves you, no matter what. Don't listen to the lie.

Another lie the Enemy uses is that if you become fully intimate with God He will make you do things you hate. This is the lie most of us fall for. God's going to send you to Africa or make you wash the feet of homeless men in an urban shelter. He's going to make you a fanatical street preacher warning that the world is coming to an end. That doesn't make any sense at all, but we imagine that will be our assignment and so we hide out in the Kingdom of Me. What I've learned is that God wants you to serve Him with the unique skills and talents He's given you. If you're a lousy public speaker, He won't call you to be a preacher. Or if He does, He'll not only transform you into a polished speaker but also give you a love for preaching. That's just the way God works.

There is no secret formula for allowing God to live where He belongs—deep inside of you. Believe that He is there. Ask yourself regularly just how much of Him you are allowing into your soul. Take time to be still and know, and eventually the question of where

God is becomes a nonissue. You know He's right there. The more you relax and enjoy God's presence in you, the easier it becomes to lower the barriers that keep Him out. The moments and hours and days of pure intimacy create a longing for more.

A Taste of His Consuming Presence

In the summer of 1987 I was working as an intern with Proctor & Gamble. I had spent a couple of days out in Los Angeles doing focus groups with housewives, trying to determine why they bought Bounty paper towels in places like Sam's Club and Target versus their local grocery store. I know that's hysterical, but I was working on the Bounty paper towel brand, and consumer behavior really was fascinating to me. After my meetings, I boarded a Boeing 767 at LAX to fly to Cincinnati. As usual, the plane headed west out over the Pacific Ocean before circling back east. About two minutes after takeoff, while still over the ocean, everyone in the plane heard something you never want to hear on a jet: silence. Then we heard something else you never want to hear when you're flying: the flight attendant's voice—businesslike yet with a tinge of concern: "Ladies and gentlemen, the pilot is aware that the engines are silent." Then within about five to ten seconds another announcement, this one more urgent: "We need to prepare for a crash landing. Please look under your seats; put on your life jackets."

The whole plane just went crazy. Passengers began screaming and yelling. Mass confusion ensued. The woman sitting next to me began shouting, "I can't die! I can't die!" In an instant my whole mind went hot. There was a burning sensation that went through my whole body, which was probably a huge surge of adrenaline. But when I realized that this was it—that my life was about to end—I experienced a level of intimacy with God that I've never experienced again in that way. I felt as though I were looking at God face to face and sensing from Him how He saw me without all my pretense: He loved me so much.

All my layers of protection, of pretending to be competent and confident, were stripped away. I was revealed completely to God. He revealed my true self and showed me that He did not see those layers. Never saw them. He saw to the root of who I was. My unprotected self, the self I tried to hide from others. And in that instant, I felt no shame. None at all. In fact, I felt relief.

He was not buying the whole act. He knew who I really was and He loved me anyway. Loved me in a profound way. Not because of what I did or how good I was. He just loved me. I felt His love. I felt utterly exposed and utterly safe at the same time. That moment was a gift. I knew I could not fool God, although part of me thought I had been, if I am honest with myself. Without knowing it, I had been trying to impress God and in some ways protect myself from Him. The walls I had built up to create my own kingdom were actually walls that kept me away from Him.

He knew who I was and He wanted me anyway. My false self was revealed, and He showed me that the person He created was the one He loved. And it was okay to just be me. No pretense. No hiding. No need to protect. I could let Him in all the way because He knew me and saw me as I was, naked and exposed.

I felt a profound sense of intimacy. To have someone see you fully, all the way to the very core of your being, and to fully, 100 percent accept and love you anyway. And that someone was God Himself. He adored me. He had nothing but love for me. I knew my life was over. I was trained as an engineer. I was strapped into a Boeing 767 filled with fuel, we were free-falling from the sky with no engine power, and we weren't very far off the ground. The reality was obvious, but I was at peace. I was, in the midst of that chaotic plane, still. I was peaceful and aware of God.

I was going home (and it wasn't Texas).

As the plane continued its rapid descent, I quickly put on my life jacket and helped the lady next to me with hers. By now she was praying out loud, so I looked her in the eyes and said, "You keep praying and I'll take care of you." And we just sat there waiting to hit the water and explode when the pilot's voice came over the loudspeaker: "Ladies and gentlemen, everything's fine. Sorry about that." Seriously, that's what he said: "Sorry." With everyone screaming, I had not heard the engines roar back to life. And then, as if this were not that big a deal (which it was), the plane climbed, then turned back toward the land flying the five hours to Cincinnati, Ohio.

When we finally landed and I got back to the house I was renting,

I went to my bedroom, laid down on my bed, and started to weep. Mostly because almost dying in a plane crash had been such a terrifying experience. But also because I experienced a moment with God where I glimpsed the deep intimacy that He longs to enjoy with me.

THE SHIFT IN ACTION

So how can we make this shift? How can we experience God's presence in a deep way so that we begin to think "we" instead of "me"?

It begins with this simple phrase: "Be still and know." Too often we are running too fast; our lives are frantic. Through the words of Psalm 46, God invites us to "be still, and know that I am God" (verse 10). We must choose to change our actions from hurry and franticness to stillness. We must regularly choose to be still and simply know that God is with us, that He loves us. We must move the focus from "me" to God, to knowing that He loves us and is for us.

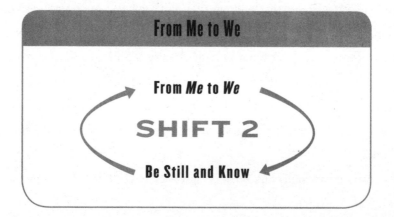

From Me to We

From *Me* to *We*

SHIFT 2

Be Still and Know

Even in the chaos of that plane that I thought was headed for a nosedive into the ocean, I felt a stillness and serenity. I knew God's love. If we want to know God in that way when we are in a moment of panic, we have to choose to experience it and practice it regularly in our ordinary days.

According to our research, people who experience God's presence do so by spending time alone with God where they can be still and know. Relational intimacy is built by spending time with someone. Spending quiet moments one on one with another person, especially if you do it frequently, not only builds connection but also makes you start to think in terms of "we" instead of "me."

Those quiet moments fill you and strengthen you. I'm not talking about a prayer time where you tell God what you need—although that's fine. I'm talking about taking time to simply be still. To be in God's loving presence. These quiet, undemanding moments remind you that you're loved, even when you're not accomplishing and achieving. However, they can be hard to find in this busy, noisy world. And even when you do find the time, you sometimes wonder if doing so is worth it, because you may not have a profound experience every time—they are often just ordinary moments in which you are quietly aware of God's love and presence. However, over time, taking time to be still and know will connect you to God in a deep way. Those quiet moments will provide a reservoir to draw on in difficult moments. If you've never experienced feeling peace and love in a quiet place with God, you're a lot less likely to experience it when you're on a plane hurtling toward the ocean.

"Be still and know" is an action that feels, ironically, like a lack of action, so it's hard for us. We are oriented toward action, doing, tasks. We even think of our quiet time as something we have to "do," reading a certain passage or praying for a certain amount of time.

As we slow down and simply are still with God, spending time in His presence, we ask ourselves, *Where is God right now? Is He close or far away?* And if it seems He is far off, we invite God to show

Sam's Story

My wife and I had been doing mission work in Central Mexico for eleven years, and we were looking for our next step. Where was God calling us? I intentionally got away to the beach to pray about it. And I had this moment, alone with God, where He didn't necessarily tell me what to do, but I just had a deep sense of peace. As much as I wanted an answer, this was much better. I had, in that moment, a sense that this connection with God, this peace, was how I was supposed to live.

During most of my life, I wanted more of God for all the wrong reasons. I wanted Him to make me a better leader, a better pastor. To help me achieve my objectives, goals, and visions. But things have changed. Now I simply want Him for the sake of being with Him, as it was in that moment at the beach. I am not doing this to get something; I am doing this to be with Him. I want to lose myself in that more and more.

us what is stopping us from letting Him in and experiencing the reality that He is right there. In stillness, we come face to face not only with God but also with ourselves. In that quiet moment, we see that we've been busy building barricades that keep God at a distance.

When we get quiet and alone with God, we move closer to God. We become aware of the God who is already as close as the air we breathe and who loves us so much. We stop asking, "Where is God?" and get quiet enough to realize He's been there all along. We invite Him to speak, and we listen. We invite Him to show us what's stopping us from moving closer to Him, what's preventing intimacy with Him. He does not need to come closer; He is as close as can be. We are the ones who need to open ourselves to His presence and let Him all the way in.

REFLECT

My heart has heard you say, "Come and talk with me."
And my heart responds, "Lord, I am coming."
(Psalm 27:8, NLT)

But I have calmed and quieted myself,
I am like a weaned child with its mother;
like a weaned child I am content. (Psalm 131:2)

What keeps you from taking the time to stop and just be with God, with no agenda other than to be with Him?

 ## REMEMBER

Each day, find time to be still, even if it's only for five minutes. Remember that God is *here* with you, not out *there.* Pay attention to when you think "me" (or "I") and mentally replace it with "we."

CHAPTER 7

From Head
to Heart

As we move from the Kingdom of Me and become more deeply aware that God is not just nearby but in us, we find ourselves pulled in two directions. We love experiencing intimacy with God, having God in us all the time, thinking of "we" instead of "me." But as much as we love that relationship, we are, as the old hymn says, "prone to wander." Or, as the apostle Paul lamented, we do the things we don't want to do and struggle to do the things we know are right, no matter how much we want to do them (see Romans 7:15).

What shifts need to happen to keep us from wandering? What actions facilitate and reinforce those shifts in our thinking?

I don't know about you, but I was brought up in a very intellectual faith. Reason and rationality were high values, both in the culture and in the church. Being "smart" was important. Now, reason and intellect are wonderful gifts, but focusing on them exclusively can keep us in our heads and prevent us from engaging our hearts. And yet, this is the shift we must make—from our heads to our hearts—if we want to access a life of more. We don't abandon our intellect, but we augment it with a depth of feeling and experience that happens when we engage our hearts.

Surprisingly, the practice that facilitates this shift is engagement with the Bible. Most of us who grew up in the church, especially evangelical churches, tend to think of the Bible in terms of intellectual analysis, or study. And study is important. But there is much more to interaction with the Bible. Those people living a life of more have a multifaceted approach to Scripture.

Our research was very clear: people who were closest to God interacted with the Bible every day, or nearly every day. They read, studied, reflected, memorized. More compelling than their habit was their motive: they seemed hungry for God and saw the Bible as just as essential to their lives as food. They studied, but their engagement went beyond intellect to what can only be described as deep, hungering love.

When I was growing up, my mom would advise me, "Eat something good every day." It's a healthy habit, an action that will shift our physical health. I like to think about engaging with the Bible as "eating something good every day." That's the action that reinforces the shift from head to heart. The Bible encourages us to feast on God's Word. Jesus said we don't live on bread alone but on God's words and truth (see Matthew 4:4). Taking in God's words, digesting them, and letting them be the means of growth and change is an essential shift in action that will lead to a life of more.

Engaging with the Bible not only draws us closer to God but also enables us to love others more deeply. We can share the feast, so to speak. In Ezekiel 3:10–11, God told His prophet, "Son of man, let all my words sink deep into your own heart first. Listen to them carefully for yourself. Then go to your people in exile and say to them, 'This is what the Sovereign LORD says!' Do this whether they listen to you or not" (NLT). If we want to help others, we've got to feast on God's Word first. We have to let God's Word sink deep into our hearts before we can speak truth into the lives of others.

As I studied leaders who had let God's Word sink deep into their hearts, I admired their love for Scripture, their deep commitment to study and reflection. I had long made a habit of reading and even memorizing Scripture. But I knew some folks who simply lit up when they talked about the Bible, and I knew I didn't. Sure, reading God's Word brought great insights and strengthened my relationship with God. Memorizing Scripture was a helpful practice. As a pastor, I even had opportunities to teach God's Word—and I really enjoyed doing that. Engaging with the Bible was a good thing, but I knew it didn't turn my crank the way it did for some people. To me it was simply a discipline—an obligation that occasionally brought me joy or insight.

I didn't fully "get it" until the love of my life, my wife, Lynn, quietly began a spiritual practice that changed both of our lives.

WHEN MY WIFE FELL IN LOVE

While I was immersed in the research to understand how people grew closer to God, Lynn began spending more time in the Bible: studying it, memorizing it, and talking about it in more passionate terms than I had ever heard from her before. She and some friends had joined a local study called *The Bible in 90 Days** at the Lutheran church across the street from where we lived. If you read twelve pages of the Bible every day, you can read the entire Bible in ninety days, and that's what she set out to do. I had seen—even tried to participate—in programs that get you through the Bible in a year, so I confess I wasn't all that impressed with what I assumed was just another Bible-reading plan.

The ninety-day plan was not meant to make her a Bible expert or scholar. Rather, she immersed herself in the story and was able to get an overview of God's overarching plan for His people and their redemption. If something jumped off the page, she might study it later. But the idea was simply to experience the story, day in and day out.

The amazing thing about this exercise is how it transformed her. My wife has loved Jesus for a long time. She's studied the Bible for much of her life. She's done countless studies and classes, learned in small groups, and so on, to increase her understanding of God's Word and will. She is a woman who lives her faith and is committed to spiritual growth. Her walk with Christ is one of the things that attracted me to her and that I continue to admire and respect.

But this particular exercise brought a change that was different from anything she'd ever experienced. Immersion in God's Word changed her in ways that surprised both of us.

As I watched my wife dig into the Bible for about forty-five min-

---

* Ted Cooper Jr.: http://scriptureawakening.com/

utes every day, I could sense something extraordinary. My children saw her reading every day. I saw her reading every day. But what really got my attention was the way that she could hardly contain herself when she talked about the Bible.

When she got to the end of the ninety days, the children and I celebrated her. We wanted to honor her for having the discipline to read the entire Bible in such a short period of time. We were all excited, but Lynn seemed a bit wistful. She said her main reaction when she got to the end was sadness because it was over. Something profound had changed inside of her—something so deep and attractive that, to be honest, I became a little envious, but in a good way. She had fallen in love with the Bible.

A few months after her ninety-day Bible reading experience, Lynn decided to sign up for a year-long scripture-memory program with best-selling author and popular speaker Beth Moore. The program offered an incentive: if you memorized a verse every fifteen days for a year, and thus memorized twenty-four Bible verses, you'd win free admission to a Beth Moore event. Lynn signed on with a friend, and I decided that I wanted to do it with her.

On the first and fifteenth of each month we each picked a verse to commit to memory, and then we shared why we picked that verse. Those became some of the most extraordinarily intimate conversations we had ever had in our marriage. Diving into those verses affected me profoundly. During my workdays, I would go for a brief walk in a quiet hallway and recite my memory verses out loud. Powerful insights flowed from immersing myself in those scriptures and living with them daily. I felt God speaking the words directly into my heart. Something really different was going on in me; my soul felt as if it were coming alive in a new way.

I, too, was falling in love with God's Word. Engaging with Scripture shifted from something I should do to something I craved, wanted, hungered for.

I couldn't get enough, and yet, paradoxically, I found the Bible immensely satisfying. At the same time that I was doing the Bible memory program, I decided I would also try the ninety-day plan Lynn had already done. I had been a Christian since I was a child and was now in a position of leadership at a wonderful church, but I don't think I had ever read the Bible straight through from Genesis to Revelation.

You probably know people who seem to have a gift of interacting with the Bible. They seem to absolutely *love* the Bible. They love reading it. They love studying it. They love talking about it. And they "eat" of it as if it were the most nourishing and delicious soul food they've ever had.

Now, I believed the Bible was God's inspired Word and contained wisdom and instruction that would help me live a better life. I could read it and apply it to my life, which would help me live more closely to God. If things weren't going as well as they should for me, I could dip into the Bible and find a little pep talk to pick me up. But to be perfectly honest, I didn't love it. I didn't have that intimate relationship with it, and while I thought it would be nice to view the Bible that way, I told myself that passion like others had was a spiritual gift reserved for those who taught the Bible. I didn't have that gift. End of story.

It's not that I didn't find the Bible interesting. I'd read it for years. When I was in graduate school at Stanford, a friend introduced me to Peninsula Bible Church in nearby Palo Alto, California, where I was exposed for the first time in my life to expository teaching—a verse-by-verse exploration into the meaning of the text in a way that made the Bible come alive. That experience brought the first of several shifts. The Bible moved from being a helpful ritual to something that was alive, full of emotion and feeling. The church had a team of preachers, anchored by Ray Stedman, one of the premier expository preachers of his generation. Influenced by the teaching at Peninsula Bible, I started really studying God's Word. The church published verbatim transcripts of every single sermon that was preached by their team of preachers. People could take them for free from a big rack in the lobby. So I did. Reading those sermons became my "seminary course" for becoming a better student of the Bible. Even after I moved from Stanford to Chicago I subscribed to these sermons and received a monthly package of them in the mail. (There was no Internet back then!)

What I discovered is that the more I understood about the Bible, the more I developed a hunger for it. Really studying it instead of just reading it made it come alive inside of me. But I knew there was more to the Bible. I saw it in other friends who were passionate about the Bible the way a gourmet is passionate about food.

As I interviewed leaders of many dynamic churches, I found

they exhibited a depth of intimacy with God and His Word that was almost magnetic. It was one of the most attractive things I've ever seen, and it made me wonder: Do you really have to have a spiritual gift of teaching to fall in love with the Bible? I saw leaders who were in love with God's Word, and I wanted the same thing. They had something I did not have, and in a virtuous way, I wanted it. I wanted it badly. I just didn't know how to do it. How do you fall in love with the Bible?

That was my mind-set when I began the ninety-day Bible reading. I frankly didn't expect that to change. I just saw how profoundly the experience had impacted my wife, Lynn, and I thought it would perhaps help me appreciate the Bible a little more.

So I started from the beginning. Yes, there are parts of the Old Testament that get a little boring or tedious, but reading the whole story of God and us reveals God's character and love. You see this pattern in the Old Testament of God refusing to give up on His people, even when they reject Him. You see how badly God wants to be close to His people. And His people were fickle! Read Judges 3–4 if you want examples of how God forgave His people over and over. You see the ache in His heart for people, even when they turned away from Him. God's Word just keeps hammering home to your heart that God will not give up on people. No matter how far they fell away from Him, ignored Him, even rejected Him, He always forgave them and welcomed them back.

The most astonishing part of the experience occurred when I finished the Old Testament and dove into the New Testament. It was amazing to hear how different the words of Jesus sounded compared to all the words of the Old Testament. All the words from the ancient kings and prophets, the words of Isaiah, Moses, David, Solomon, all the great voices of the Old Testament paled in comparison to the way that Jesus's voice rang true. He spoke with authority, yet with great wisdom and love. He reached out to those whom others had abandoned or scorned. His heart was deeply touched by the poor and needy, and when He came upon the sick, He healed them. Reading about Jesus in the context of the entire Bible caused Him to stand out as the true Son of God who came as one of us. Reading the Bible as one narrative, you see the whole plan unfold and then get to the end in the book of Revelation where again, He doesn't abandon us. He's always there for us.

My ninety-day deep dive into the Bible changed me, and it forever changed the way I see Scripture. I now know, deep in my soul, in even a visceral way, that God is always pursuing *me*. Immersing myself in the Bible—reading it from beginning to end—made God's words come alive for me. Suddenly I found myself in love with the Bible. Deeply in love.

Although reading through the Bible is in part an intellectual exercise, Bible engagement actually perpetuates an important shift, moving our relationships with God from our heads to our hearts. It's what happened to me in my ninety-day experience, and it is what happens to those who decide to engage fully and regularly with the Bible.

When we shift from inside to outside, from "me" to "we," as we discussed in previous chapters, those things happen because of an act of our will. We decide that we will leave our own kingdoms. We consciously think about changing our language from "me" to "we." And our attitudes and actions change as a result.

When we read the Bible from outside the box, we change our perspective. Instead of trying to figure out how the words can help me with my life (inside-the-box thinking), we view them for instructions for outside-the-box living. We stop thinking about the Bible as a guide that can help me to provide for and/or protect *myself,* and we shift to seeing it as a guide that will help us engage with *others* out in the world. We begin to view the Bible as a map for living outside the box.

And it's when we fall in love with the Bible that we begin to experience more of God. It's when we shift from our heads (thinking about the Bible) to our hearts (falling in love with the Bible) that we move closer to living a life of more.

What the Research Showed

When we studied half a million church attenders to find out what kinds of practices they engaged in, the research was very clear: the number one practice that catalyzes movement toward deeper intimacy with God is reading, studying, reflecting upon, and even memorizing truth from the Bible. They ate something good every day.

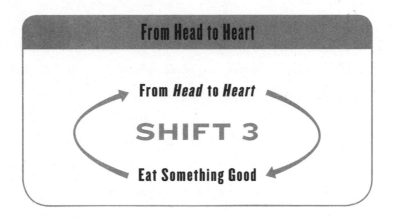

Hunger for More

Some people like to think of engaging the Bible as a habit, and I suppose that's okay. Bible reading could indeed be a good habit to develop. But I really prefer the idea of the Bible as "food" or nutrition that is essential to having an intimate relationship with God. Eating isn't a habit; it's absolutely necessary to live. A habit is something you can break or give up. You simply cannot live without food, and that's how you should approach the Bible: *I need this to survive. Without it I will die.*

Many people tend to label the Bible as an instruction manual or a rule book. But if you actually read it, you'll see that it is much more like a love letter than a rule book. It's a feast for your soul, not something you choke down because it's supposed to be good for you.

The key is not to just snack on the Bible but to consume it with the same eagerness and expectation that you bring to a seven-course gourmet meal. God's words to you given in the Bible truly are food for your life. As Jesus reminded us in the only sermon of His recorded in the Bible, "Blessed are those who hunger and thirst for righteousness, for they will be filled" (Matthew 5:6). That's what we long for—to be filled so completely by God. And one of the ways that happens is by immersing ourselves in the words He lovingly gave us. We don't just read them, but we savor them, reflect on them, and let them shape everything in our whole being. That's how we can pursue and maintain intimacy with God. We want His words to preoccupy us. We want them to overwhelm us with wisdom, encouragement, and instruction all day long.

When we read and reflect on the Bible regularly, it provides strength, like a healthy meal. Strength to battle the distractions that can injure our relationship with God. Strength to choose to live in God's kingdom rather than our own. Each day we're inundated with words and messages—a flood of information that can easily crowd God's words out of our lives. Think of how many times you look at your cell phone. I've had conversations with people who were constantly interrupted by a blip or buzz from their phone, indicating an e-mail or a text was awaiting them. I've done it myself. We are so easily distracted, assaulted by messages 24/7 from e-mail, texts, Twitter, Facebook, radio programs, and television shows. Hey, I love the Internet and all the technology that allows us to do so many phenomenal things, but if we're not careful, we can become consumed by all these messages and images aimed at our brains. All these words and images pummel us with the velocity of a wide-open fire hydrant, threatening to drown out the still, small whisper of God that reminds us that we are loved.

We must counter those words with God's words.

And when it comes to full intimacy with God, reading His words isn't enough. We must consume them. Or as Eugene Peterson described in *Eat This Book,* "Reading that enters our souls as food enters our stomachs, spreads through our blood, and becomes holiness and love and wisdom."* This is not the way most of us have learned to read the Bible, but if want to move to that next level of full intimacy with God, that's how we should approach His words to us.

If you do only one thing to put God at the center of your being—to allow Him to be *in* you rather than out there—the research shows that the most effective strategy is to engage the Bible. Feast on His words. Eat the Bible as you would a great meal.

QUALITY AND QUANTITY

When our children were young, I remember hearing busy parents say the *quantity* of time spent with children did not matter as long as the *quality* was high. When it comes to engaging the Bible in a way that cultivates deeper intimacy with God, you need both. Grabbing a few verses here and there won't cut it. Both the research and my own personal experience suggest that you need to read parts of the Bible each day, and you also need to spend time thinking and

---

* Eugene H. Peterson, *Eat This Book: A Conversation in the Art of Spiritual Reading* (Grand Rapids, MI: Eerdmans, 2006), 4.

meditating on what you just read. I know that may be difficult for busy people, but that's the point.

The key is to immerse yourself in the Bible. But what does that mean? I hesitate to try to spell out a specific plan for consuming the Bible, because everyone is different. What works for me may not work that well for you. However, the following principles can be adapted to your particular rhythms of life.

Read through the entire Bible, from beginning to end. Dipping into it here or there is kind of like sampling a meal. You really need to consume the whole thing. Take a year if you need to, though I found the ninety-day experience breathtaking. Just stick with it, especially through those parts that may seem confusing or even a little boring. It's important to see the entire narrative of God's interaction with His people.

Read every day. Not in a legalistic sense. There may be days when you don't read at all. Don't punish yourself—just get caught up the next day. Or the next. Remember, it's food. Try to eat something good every day. Sometimes you miss the dinner bell or have to skip a meal, which only makes you hungrier for the next one. If you keep at it you will soon develop a hunger for the Word that drives you back to it if you happen to miss a "meal." The key is to set aside some time every day when you can read the Bible unrushed and uninterrupted.

Reflect on what you read. This is probably the most important part of reading the Bible in order to come into full intimacy with God. Here's the thing: you can't reflect in a hurry. Most of us need to slow down when it comes to Scripture. The Bible is not fast food; it is not meant to be gulped, but rather savored. Tasted and delighted in. You need to chew and actually taste your food.

The Benedictine monks handed down a practice known as *lectio divina* that many Christians use to engage the Bible. Very simply, it consists of four parts or steps in reading the Bible: read, meditate, pray, and contemplate. Some people will read a passage for the day and then close their eyes and open their hearts to what God might be trying to say to them through the words they just read. Ask yourself, *What did I like about the words I just consumed?* Ask God, *What do You want me to know?* Then read the text expectantly, waiting to hear from Him.

Memorize scripture that is especially inspiring or encouraging to you. This is a tough one for a lot of people, as it was for me. And yet I know people who have memorized song lyrics from their favorite singers or whole lines of dialogue from their favorite movies. It all has to do with what matters most to you. For me, the process of committing scripture to memory—imprinting it on my brain—was unbelievable. It was as if God's words were becoming a part of me. Some people find it helpful to memorize Scripture along with a familiar tune.

Note that this immersion in the Bible doesn't happen in church. Nor can it, really. You can get great Bible teaching at church, and you should. But this love affair with God's Word is more intimate than anything that can occur in church. To pursue deep intimacy with God, you need to spend time digging into the Scriptures yourself.

Your church can certainly help, and I pray and hope that you belong to a church that can help you with this through teachings in your Sunday services, classes, or small groups. But this is not something you should put on your church. This is your responsibility. As Willow Creek senior pastor Bill Hybels says, "I can't read your Bible for you."

If you long for more in your life, if you want a deeper sense of God's presence and peace, if you desire the fullness of a relationship with Him, you will find these when you feast on His Word. Ask Him to help you fall in love with His Word. Once you cross that line and develop a passionate love affair with the Bible, it will invoke a holy longing in which you desire more and more time with God.

And that will lead you to do something you've never done before and allow you to experience God in a new way. That's what we're going to explore in the next chapter.

REFLECT

> Sin speaks a dead language that means nothing to you;
> God speaks your mother tongue, and you hang on
> every word. (Romans 6:10, MSG)

> Simon Peter answered him, "LORD, to whom shall we
> go? You have the words of eternal life." (John 6:68)

Decide right now what next step you need to take to engage with the Bible. If you can't think of anything, let me suggest reading the Bible in ninety days or memorizing one verse every fifteen days. Doing nothing is not an option. You will starve.

 ## REMEMBER

Each day, read, study, reflect on, or memorize a piece of the Bible. As you go to bed, ask yourself, *Did I eat something good today?* If the answer is no, it's not too late. It will make the difference between really living or slowly starving to death.

CHAPTER 8

From Closed
to Open

We've moved from inside our little box, the Kingdom of Me, to life outside the box, in God's kingdom, and learned to say we're sorry. We've made a shift from "me" to "we," seeing ourselves as intimately connected to God, by taking time to "be still and know." We've shifted the connection with God from our heads to our hearts and reinforced and maintained that intimacy with God by engaging with the Scriptures and "eating something good every day."

These actions are essential but incomplete. God created us to be in relationship not only with Him but also with others. The movement from "me" to "we" is a movement from isolation to relationship with God and also to community with other people.

Simply put, those who live a life of more do not do it alone.

You cannot access the deepest levels of intimacy with God unless you also open your life to others in community. Deep spiritual friendships with other people will allow you to experience greater intimacy with God. This reflects the truth about how you were created: to live in community. It is not good for human beings to be alone.

Life outside the box, outside the Kingdom of Me, is a life lived with others. The shift at this stage of the journey is from closed to open, that is open to others. We do that by building a web of relationships.

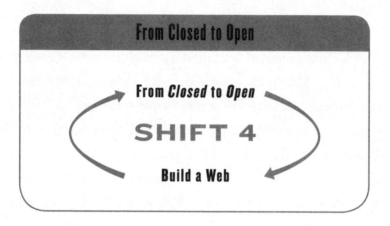

BACK TO THE BEGINNING

In the beginning when God created the world, He made light and dark, day and night, water and land, birds and animals. As He made each thing, He declared it good. Then He made man, and for the first time He said something's not right. The human being himself wasn't flawed or bad. It was his *aloneness* that was "not good." God said, "It is not good for the man to be alone. I will make a helper suitable for him" (Genesis 2:18)—not an assistant or underling, but someone just like him to stand beside him as a partner. So God created woman. Some people interpret this passage to mean that a man is not complete without a woman or a woman is not complete without a man, but I don't think that is the point. Look at the full measure of the Scriptures and you'll find that we weren't supposed to be alone, none of us. It doesn't mean we're supposed to have a mate (both Jesus and the apostle Paul were single, and Paul wrote about the advantages of being unmarried). Rather, it means we were created for community.

From the beginning we were designed to do life *together*, with our hearts knitted together with the Father and with each other. We need others to tell us the truth, to hold us accountable, to encourage us, to laugh with us, to cry with us, to rejoice with us, and to simply experience life with us.

At the beginning we had unity with God, and we had unity with each other. That's how it was supposed to be. When we broke from God and from each other, we started erecting our own walls and building our own castles to keep everyone else out. As we said earlier, when we build our own kingdoms, we have to protect and provide. So we wall others out because we see them as competitors, trying to grab the limited resources that we need to provide for ourselves. Unfortunately, this leads to isolation.

On our journeys toward a life of more, we make an important discovery: this view of others as competitors is a lie.

When we decide to move from our kingdoms to God's kingdom, we abandon our kingdoms so that we can be reunited with God. And then a curious thing happens: as we dismantle the walls around us, we open ourselves to the opportunity to experience community with others. Free from the responsibility of defending our territory, we can pursue intimacy again with others—deep friendships of unity. This is how it was supposed to be.

The Only Thing That Will Last

At the end of the day, the only thing that will last is people. The only thing that is truly immortal is the human soul. At the end of our lives, all our possessions and accomplishments will be gone. God and other people are the only things that will last into eternity. If we really lived as if this were true, we'd value people more than anything else.

This theme of unity and community runs throughout the Bible. God called Abraham to follow Him and begin a great nation—God's people (see Genesis 12:1–2). Jesus said later in Matthew 18:20, "For where two or three gather in my name, there am I with them." That's a beautiful mystery: when we come together in unity, we experience God in a way that's impossible on our own. In fact, the Bible even says, "If we love one another, God lives in us and his love is made complete in us" (1 John 4:12).

In many of his letters to churches, the apostle Paul emphasized the importance of unity in the body of Christ. In the opening verses of Ephesians 4, he talked about the unity of one body, one spirit, and one hope. Then in verses 15–16 he said, "Instead, speaking the truth in love, we will grow to become in every respect the mature body of him who is the head, that is, Christ. From him the whole body, joined and held together by every supporting ligament, grows and builds itself up in love, as each part does its work." God designed us to be interdependent—interconnected into a network of relationships.

Honestly, I've thought about this subject for almost thirty years of my adult life and it's still a mystery to me. There is still something that battles deep within me. As great as community is, as much as it feels like the way life is supposed to be, I still sometimes hold back. I feel conflicted. Everything in me understands and feels the desire to be one with other people, to be free to be myself in front of them, to trust them fully, to laugh deeply, to not be ashamed, to not worry about what other people say to me. I long for that, yet it can feel terrifying. I need to protect my soul. It feels dangerous to reveal what's going on inside of me to other people. If you've ever been hurt by someone in the past (and we all have), community can feel frightening.

I know, from research and lots of conversations, that I'm not the only one who wrestles with this. Community is amazing, and community is hard. So why bother? Why build a web?

First, we pursue biblical community because it's the way to experience life as it is supposed to be. Community is God's plan A, and there is no plan B. We all need (whether we admit it or not) a place where we can tell each other the truth. In community, we help each other break free of the messages from the culture around us— messages that tell us that we really should be building the Kingdom of Me, that we have to take care of ourselves, that others can't be trusted.

Community with others who love you and love God, others who

can tell you the truth that's anchored in God's Word, will ultimately help you live the life you're longing for. When you have friends who are willing to take a risk by telling you the truth in love, that's a profound and rare gift. When you have friends who will hear your story and affirm God's love for you, even in your brokenness, that's more than a gift—it's a lifeline.

Second, and most importantly, we are to be in relationship because God asks us to. The essence of being a follower of Jesus and a disciple is to do what God asks, which is to go make disciples of all nations. What is a disciple? As mentioned earlier, it is someone who is characterized by his or her love of others. We are meant to be a blessing to other people in our lives. We were created to give away God's love, to be people who build up, who see people, who acknowledge them and give them encouragement, who give them permission to be who they were made to be by God Himself.

A WEB OF RELATIONSHIPS

Those who live a life of more don't have only a few friends. They've worked hard to build a web of relationships that includes friends, small groups, deep friendships, and even mentoring relationships. They are continually expanding the web, building it by getting to know people and loving them.

Our research showed us that people who are living a life of more live in biblical community. They've built a web of relationships in which they give and receive. That web allows them to continually open their lives to God and others. It facilitates the shift from closed to open.

Jesus Himself lived this kind of life. And it was wonderful, and exasperating for Him as well. Jesus didn't just give to others. He needed others. He needed a few close friends. He needed a group, and then He needed others beyond those. He built a web of relationships, and we should also.

Those living a life of more have built this web of relationships. Somewhat surprisingly, their community life is not completely organized by the church. In fact, many of them are not in church-sponsored small groups, but they are in groups, have spiritual friendships, and have mentors. They have moved from organized community to organic community. They still take advantage of what the church offers, but they've gone beyond that to create community on their own.

In the rest of this chapter, we are going to look at those three types of relationships—small groups, spiritual friendships, and mentoring relationships—and how we can intentionally build those into our daily lives.

SMALL GROUPS

Small groups are a great laboratory for learning the basics of biblical community. They're a place to pursue relationships with others.

Shortly after Lynn and I got married, we joined a couples' small group where we experienced deep, life-changing community. The four other couples we met with every other week became our intimate friends. These folks prayed over Lynn and me as we struggled with infertility, and then later they celebrated with us as we dedicated our first and second child. Likewise, we shared in the struggles and joys of every other couple in the group.

After several years, three of the four couples moved away, far away, out of state, and the group dissolved. I just assumed at that point that God would bring another group to replace the one we'd lost. Sadly, that special collection of people has yet to be reassembled in our life.

Since then Lynn and I have been in other terrific, meaningful small groups. But none reached the level of intimacy and disclosure and support of that initial group. Lynn and I realize now the extraordinary gift that group was. We want to appreciate and savor intimate friendships but at the same time not hold on to them and not demand of God that He allow them to last forever.

Our research indicated that the main thing people want from a small group is a safe place to process the issues of life. To bring their lives and their stories into conversation with God and His story, to try to make sense of this world, and to try to figure out how to live in God's kingdom. Healthy groups provide this space.

These groups are essentially centered on truth, speaking the truth in love. Consequently, God's truth is shared and studied, and it becomes the reference point for the conversation. We vulnerably share our story but also talk about becoming part of God's story.

Healthy groups include study of the Bible and discussion of how it applies to the stories of the individuals in the group.

Some groups form organically. For example, if you are married with children, you're in a group: your family. A profound shift in my parenting occurred when I understood that my wife and three children are a small group where we are learning how to listen to each other, to love each other, to care for each other, and to serve each other. We're teaching our children how to be friends with one another and to encourage and love one another.

Your family will thrive as a group if you are intentional. As my children got older, I tried to apply to my family what I knew about building a good small group at a church. Your family can be a place of spiritual nourishment and safety, not just for your children but for you as well. This will look different in different stages of your children's development, but I encourage you to view your family as one of the groups that make up your web.

In groups we learn how to listen, not just to what other people are saying, but to what's going on in their hearts or under the surface. Listening is an act of love. In a healthy group, members listen to one another but also keep one ear tuned to God. And God may prompt one member to give encouragement, wisdom, a challenge, or empathy to another—and in so doing allow both of them to experience intimacy with each other and with God. When that happens, it's pretty profound. And it can be an effective catalyst for the spiritual growth of everyone in the group.

Spiritual Friendships

The second type of relationships are called spiritual friendships. As the name implies, these are friends with whom we can talk about our spiritual lives. They can include a broad range of people, from casual relationships to deep, intimate friendships. The key is to be intentional about encouraging each other to grow closer to God. Spiritual friendship is a two-way peer relationship in which we give and receive love and encouragement.

The couples' group I mentioned earlier included one couple who didn't move away—Scott and Becky. For more than a decade, Scott and I got together about three times a month to run together, share a meal, or enjoy a cup of coffee together. Those meetings always included deep, honest conversation. Scott is someone who knows everything about my life, all the secrets. He's a friend who would do anything for me, and I'd do the same for him. I can't imagine my life without that relationship. Since Lynn and I moved away from Chicago, Scott and I continue to talk by phone and we occasionally visit. We're still incredibly close. (Read more of Scott's story in the sidebar on page 149.)

You may long for this type of friendship but wonder how to find it. I'd encourage you to think beyond a few people, beyond your church small group, to build a web of relationships. You can't go through life with only a few relationships; you need a web. And others need you.

How strong and how wide is your web of relationships? It's easy to make excuses: "I don't have time!" or "I just moved!" or "I'm introverted!" or "I don't know anybody who'd want that kind of friendship." In reality, we interact with people all the time, but we sometimes settle for superficiality. We don't always look for the potential to go deeper. I'm not talking about immediately baring your soul to people—true friendships take time. And some friendships you think will go very deep will hit a plateau of intimacy that you could not have predicted at the beginning. Others go much deeper than you would have predicted. So you just have to take the risk to move toward people. You have to be, as we've said, open.

If you're married, your marriage should be a spiritual friendship. Lynn and I have been married more than twenty years. In the beginning, I was madly in love and was certain that the day we married was the pinnacle of our love. But I was wrong. Our love has deepened and intensified over the years. The impact of being transparent with someone over time, entering into his or her world and letting him or her into yours, continues to amaze me. However, this doesn't happen without effort. It is something you have to build. A marriage is a living thing. It must be tended.

It's not easy to find and maintain spiritual friendships. Sometimes we don't have the energy, we don't want to take the risk, we think we've got enough friends and can barely keep up with those! I don't think that's true. I think it's a lie, and I also think it's not good for us to imagine that we get to a point in our lives where we don't have room for more friendships. I've had conversations with people who've found that as they get older, their relational worlds actually shrink and they get lonely. That's not the way it was supposed to be.

Mentors

Spiritual friendships are between peers, but we also need relationships with people who know more than we do, and we need to offer our wisdom and help to those who are less experienced in living a life of faith. In other words, we need to have mentors, and we need to be mentors.

Our research showed that people who live a life of more seek out mentors and coaches. They humbly look for people to speak into their lives, to give them coaching and advice and wisdom. They are not closed to the advice and challenge of others; they are open to it. And they take the responsibility to do the same for others. This is a chronic need in our time.

I've worked with a ministry for twenty-somethings, and one of the crying needs in that generation is for mentors. Sadly, in all the churches we've studied, a large percentage of people who could offer wisdom and help to others simply don't offer it. They feel unqualified or have simply never been asked. That's tragic—for the church, for the young people, and for the older people!

The truth is, you've been given things in life that you need to pass on to others. Some of the best small-group leaders at Willow Creek were high school students who mentored junior high kids. If a teenager can be a mentor, anyone can. You don't have to have

Scott's Story

I often think I'm going to feel closest to God when I'm on vacation in some beautiful place, away from the stress and distraction of life. But what constantly surprises me is the way I experience closeness with God in difficult conversations with loving friends.

As a child, I was abused. The whole thing was confusing and shameful. I determined not to tell anyone. Over the years I managed the pain by being really good at controlling things and helping other people. But eventually I got to a point where I was exhausted and I felt all alone. I knew I had to deal with it.

I went on a men's retreat and decided to talk to one of the leaders I knew about what had happened. He sat and just listened. He didn't rush me. It was the first time I'd talked to anyone about it. I finally said, "Here's what happened." In that moment I was expecting the worst—I expected shock and shame. But I was surprised. There were tears, from me, but then my mentor was crying too. It was so profound.

I experienced God's love through him, through the level of care and love that was in the details, so to speak. He wasn't rushing to try to fix things or make everything okay. He listened and paid close attention to everything that I was experiencing. His response was so unexpected that I broke into this laughter, and I could not stop. The whole thing was very redemptive.

everything figured out. When Jesus said to His followers, "Go and make disciples" (Matthew 28:19), He wasn't talking only to those first followers. He was talking to us. God has entrusted us with knowledge and experiences. We have a responsibility to pass that on to other people. So who are you passing things on to these days? You may not know much, but you know a little more than someone, and mentoring that someone will help both of you!

In my own life one mentor stands above them all, my dear friend John Baldwin. I first met John in 1991. I needed help—with life. I was stuck and sad and didn't know how to move forward. John, a trained Christian therapist, was the person God used to help me live again, to discover a way to access the life that is deep inside of me. I spent a couple of intense years with John and made a lot of progress. Eventually I didn't need his help on a regular basis and just needed to check in with him maybe once or twice a year.

Then in 2008, I found myself stuck again. The tools and re-sources and the way of thinking that had helped me live over the previous decade or so were not as effective. I felt I didn't have the spiritual and emotional tools I needed to go to the next level of par-enting, of being a husband, and of being a follower of Christ. Be-cause I wanted to keep growing, I returned to seeing John on a regular basis, not so much as my therapist but more as my coach. John knew my story, understood the pain in my life, had a working knowledge of how life normally tripped me up, and throughout it all reminded me of the truth. He reminded me of what's true about

God and what's true about me, and he gave me a measure of hope and lightness that you can't even imagine. I say "gave" because John died a few years ago. If this book is giving you any encouragement or hope, you have John Baldwin to thank.

REFLECT

You are all children of the light and children of the day. . . . Encourage one another and build each other up, just as in fact you are doing. (1 Thessalonians 5:5, 11)

Therefore confess your sins to each other and pray for each other so that you may be healed. The prayer of a righteous person is powerful and effective. (James 5:16)

How easy is it for you to let others into your life? Does the thought of it completely overwhelm you or excite you?

REMEMBER

Each day, decide to open yourself to the people in your life, looking for those who can become part of your relational web. You need them and they need you.

CHAPTER 9

Once we've truly chosen to let God be King, to get out of our box and live in God's kingdom, we're kind of out of a job. We are no longer kings and queens responsible for providing for and protecting our little kingdoms. Strictly speaking, we are unemployed. So what do we do with our time, our lives? What's our job? Do we even have a job? God makes it very clear: "So now I am giving you a new commandment: Love each other. Just as I have loved you, you should love each other" (John 13:34, NLT). Our job in God's kingdom is simple. We are to love people.

But the kind of love God has in mind is not about having nice warm thoughts and feelings toward others. Those are fine, but God is calling us toward something much more tangible, meaningful, and fierce. To love, in God's economy, means to serve others. *Well, that doesn't sound so bad,* you might be thinking. *I already do that. I serve at my church. I help my neighbor. I care for my spouse and children.* I'm sure you do. I know I prided myself on how I helped out my wife and children and how I was available to my friends and neighbors. I thought of myself as a loving person. But God showed me the truth a few years ago on a hot summer's day. The truth about me and the truth about love.

DEAD MAN MOWING

I was mowing my grass on one of the rare one-hundred-degree days in Chicago. As I got to the backyard, I rehashed an argument I had earlier that day with my wife. It was one of those small, everyday disagreements that escalated from small to medium the more I stewed over it, walking back and forth across the lawn. I was hurt. I wallowed in a combination of sadness, anger, and frustration—mostly because I felt that I wasn't understood.

And then out of the blue, a phrase came to mind—words that I had never thought before. It was as clear as it was simple: *Why are you so upset? You're dead.*

At first, I was confused. *What do you mean I'm dead? I'm not dead. I'm mowing the lawn. I'm breathing.* I thought maybe the heat was getting to me and heatstroke was setting in. But as I reflected on what had happened earlier with my wife, I realized that the only reason I got so upset was because I didn't get my way. I didn't get what my egocentric self wanted. Suddenly, I knew God was speaking to me. "You're dead" is not something you make up based on wishful thinking. So I paid attention.

And then I saw clearly that I could not love Lynn the way she should be loved because I was too focused on protecting myself. Too focused on getting my own way. Too obsessed by being right. (Sounds a whole lot like Kingdom-of-Me living, doesn't it?) And I knew that something needed to change. Not in Lynn, but in me.

As I continued mowing, I wondered, *What would really happen if that egocentric part of me ended right now? What if I just put to rest that part of me who wants things my own way and really surrendered all of my life, every bit of it, to God?*

I was a few days short of my fiftieth birthday. I started reflecting nostalgically on all the good I had experienced in my life. My life had been blessed. I always had meaningful work and good friends. I had traveled around the world, eaten in some great restaurants, bought a few nice cars. I've had just about everything I've ever really wanted. I married the love of my life and had three great children. And then the thought came to mind, *Fifty years is long enough to be focused on yourself.* I was at peace. Ready to "die." Then I imagined a tombstone with my name on the top and the dates 1962–2012 below. At that moment, I was marking the end of a life lived mostly for me.

I began weeping, and tears mixed with sweat that was now pouring down my face. Even though I was outside and my neighbors could see, I didn't care. It didn't matter. I just let the tears flow as I mourned the loss of my life. I gave myself a good minute or two to feel sad and to grieve and to remember. I remember thinking the sadness was good. It was a healthy response that should be felt when you realize you've lost something of value. My egocentric life—a life that was good and that I enjoyed—had died. I was putting it aside so that I could make room for others in my life.

It's not like this was the first time I ever considered unselfishness as an option. There had been other times in my life when I surrendered *parts* of my life to God's direction and will. Though I'd struggled and felt a sense of loss with those previous steps, I'd never felt this level of grief before. This was different. This was a deep sadness.

As I finished mowing I thought, *What if I just lived as though I'm dead?* Dead people don't need anything. If you don't need anything, you don't argue about whether you are right or wrong with your extraordinary wife. You don't worry about things like being late or protecting something that's important to you. Being dead means you've got a lot of time on your hands, so you don't have to rush. When you get your egocentric little self out of the way, it's amazing how it changes your outlook and opens up an entirely new world.

I remember walking through the kitchen after I finished mowing the lawn and showering. I was focused on another item on my to-do list when my daughter said, "Daddy, can I show you something?" In a split second several things happened. First, I thought, *I don't have time for this right now.* But then the second thought came equally fast: *You're dead. You don't need anything.* So I turned and gave my daughter my full attention, willingly and joyfully.

As I was listening to her tell me all about the thing most important to her at the moment, I felt myself slowing down. I was in no rush. The thing I needed to do would get accomplished (it did). The most important thing now was this moment with my daughter. I felt like what I was offering her was not my attention but my love. In that moment I felt I was loving her in a way I had never loved her before.

Over the next few days, I found this pattern repeating itself.

When people asked something from me, I would hesitate, not wanting to give it to them at that moment, and then I'd remember, *I'm dead,* and proceed to serve them (i.e., love them) the best I could. But then God showed me something that completed the picture for me. What these people needed from me was not "me," the self-focused king of my own defunct kingdom, because "I" had nothing of real value to offer them. What these people needed was a word, a touch, a look from God Himself, because that is the only thing of any real value. If I think I know what they need, I'm delusional. I have to ask God to show me truth and then to direct my actions.

So I adjusted my pattern, and when I got to the point when I remembered that I'm dead, I would give people my attention and then ask God privately, *What do You want to give this person?* Or said another way, *How do You want to love this person through me?*

Our job is to love, which means to serve, which means to die.

The shift from full to empty is facilitated by a shift in actions represented by the simple but challenging phrase, "Love. Serve. Die."

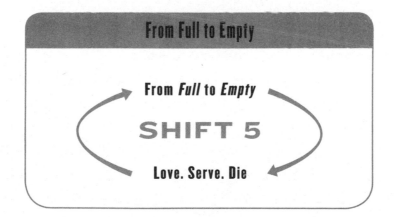

Loving Others as God Loves Them

Love. Serve. Die. What does that mean? Service might mean volunteering at a church or community organization, but just as often, it means simply having a mind-set of serving people we encounter each day.

Serving others begins with those who are close in—our family, friends, people we see every day. People we rub shoulders with every day may appear to have it all together, but often their smiles mask crushing burdens they carry alone. A life of more comes when we see them as God does. We have to ask, throughout our day, *Who am I loving in this moment? Who has God put right in front of me, whether that's the cashier at the drugstore, the waiter at a restaurant, my daughter, son, wife, or work colleague?* We must choose to be attentive in that moment, not only to see who is in front of us, but also to recognize how we can serve him or her.

Not an Easy Shift to Make

In the research, we discovered something that illustrates how hard it is to love others. As people moved from Group 1 all the way to Group 4, their self-reported love of God increased over 520 percent. That wasn't too surprising, and it made sense. The closer you get to God, the more you experience His love, resulting in loving feelings toward Him in return. Now we imagined that people who were filled with God's love would increasingly be loving toward others, and they are. When asked about their love of others, the change from Group 1 to Group 4 was 197 percent. While still very large, this increase was proportionately much less than the increase in their love for God. That really puzzled us because one would imagine that if people's love for God is increasing so rapidly and they have more of God, then obviously they would also be loving others more.

As I pondered this gap, I speculated that it has to do with not fully living outside the box. It is challenging to shift from living "full" lives where we keep all of God's love for us (in a way, almost hoarding the love we receive from God) to being willing to "empty" ourselves every single day. It can take awhile for our love for people to catch up with our love for God.

Giving away God's love is risky because we're not sure if we'll ever get any more. We have to trust God to replenish what He's given us, and that's scary. But it's when we give away that love that God replenishes it. It takes people awhile to learn that, to get to that point. So they'll grow in their love for God before they grow in their love for people.

When we looked further at Group 4, those living a life of more, they did indeed report a much higher love for others. At the same time, when asked, "Are you willing to risk everything that is important in your life for Jesus Christ?" they responded, "I'm willing to die. I'm willing to lay down everything that is important to me for the sake of Christ." That's the practice of service, taken to a new level.

The response was clear: to love what is important to God you have to be willing to lose what is important to you. People who live a life of more move from living with the love of God stored up in their box to living outside the box where they give away God's love every day.

That gentle (okay, not so gentle) whisper in my ear when I was mowing the lawn simply reiterated a recurring theme in the New Testament. We're all familiar with the words of John 3:16: "For God so loved the world that he gave his one and only Son, that whoever believes in him shall not perish but have eternal life." That verse is so comforting because it promises life. Now here's another John 3:16—actually 1 John 3:16: "This is how we know what love is: Jesus Christ laid down his life for us. And we ought to lay down our lives for our brothers and sisters." It couldn't be clearer than that.

People matter so much to Jesus that He gave His life for them. He invites us to experience that same level of love for people by calling us to be willing to love, serve, and die. In John 15:13, Jesus Himself said, "Greater love has no one than this: to lay down one's life for one's friends." Then in Philippians 2:5–8, we are called to mimic the attitude of Jesus, who, despite being the Son of God, "made himself nothing by taking the very nature of a servant." He humbled Himself and, out of love for people, allowed Himself to die a horrible death on a cross. It is a tough image, but if we seek His fullness, we have to adopt that same attitude of being willing to die for the sake of others. In Galatians 2:20 we read, "I have been crucified with Christ and I no longer live, but Christ lives in me." That's a challenging idea: to no longer live. When I die to myself and have Christ living in me—fully consuming me and fully intimate with me—I can then love what matters most to God: people.

This is a real shift in the way we normally think and the way we typically act. We think of loving someone as giving of ourselves. But Jesus says we have to die to ourselves. If we really want to take loving another person seriously, we have to get out of the way. There needs to be less of us and more of God, and we don't like that. It goes against everything we believe about ourselves. The truth is, we might be a little reluctant to love and serve and not get any credit for it. We've worked all our lives to become better people, and now He says we have to die?

Maybe one of the reasons this world is still so messed up is because even those who love God still don't really love what matters most to God. We'll give a little to others, but not everything. We're unwilling to empty ourselves so that there's nothing left but God loving through us. I don't say this to shame anybody—I do the exact same thing. Perhaps it's because we don't completely trust God's abundance, God's ability to replenish us when we empty ourselves completely. If we want the life that is truly life, we have to make a shift from full to empty so God's love can flow through.

LOVE CLOSE IN

The Bible says we've got to be faithful with a little before we're given a bigger assignment. We have to love the people right in front of us and then move outward to those we don't know. Love starts close in.

Reflect for a minute or two on the people you've encountered this week. Start with your family. How might your relationships with your spouse and your children change if you consistently put their needs ahead of yours? If you didn't just tell them that you loved them but showed them by serving them? What about that phone call where you see the number and know it's someone so needy as to be annoying? What if you took the call, listened carefully to what he or she said, and then offered to help? Not because you want to impress that person with your kindness but because it's an opportunity for God's love to flow through you as you offer the service of listening?

You're only a conduit, and that's enough when you live fully in God's kingdom rather than yours. We often assume that if we engage in character formation—trying to be good, trying to be kinder, better people—we'll access a life of more and we'll be more loving. And we'll have more peace, more love, more satisfaction. While character formation does make us feel a little bit better about ourselves, staying on that path will not help us get more out of life because the paradox is this: a life of more comes from less of you. We don't engage in the practice of service as a means of self-improvement. We serve in response to God's love for us. It's completely counterintuitive but it's true.

LOVE EXPANDS

In our research, those who reported the highest levels of love for God also, over time, reported higher levels of love for family and friends, as well as higher levels of love for strangers—people outside of their normal circles. We can sometimes romanticize the idea of loving the poor or helping the starving children in Africa.

Over time as we are faithful to loving those in our immediate circles, God will entrust us to love others we don't know. But love starts close in and then expands.

As we open our hearts to the pain in the world, we will discover just how sufficient God's love is. When we give ourselves away more and more, it does hurt. But eventually our hearts fill even more with God's love, and that is the journey of this life.

As we love in small ways, love expands, and in that expansion we'll discover our calling. Frederick Buechner, in his book *Wishful Thinking: A Seeker's ABC,* wrote, "The place God calls you to is the place where your deep gladness and the world's deep hunger meet."* And the world's deep hunger is often represented in their pain. As we move into the pain, the only way to deal with that is with God's love. God's love is the source of our gladness and our source of fulfillment, and it's the intersection of those two things. God has designed us for this.

If we haven't learned how to love on a small scale those He puts in our everyday lives, how in the world will we be able to love others? What we'll be tempted to do is love them out of our own strength and then we'll fall flat on our faces, exhausted. We'll make no impact whatsoever because the only way to deal with the pain of the world

---

* Frederick Buechner, *Wishful Thinking: A Seeker's ABC,* rev. ed. (San Francisco: HarperOne, 1993), 95.

is with the love of God, not with any human effort. We have to build that capacity to love and to give away God's love; in order to build that capacity, we have to start close in.

My wife, Lynn, almost goes too far when it comes to opening her heart to the pain of others. In fact, there have been times when I've cautioned her that she needs to create boundaries or walk away from a person she has invited into her life. Her response: "That's just not an option. These people really matter to God. Are you suggesting I just cut them off and leave them?"

I've learned by observing Lynn and talking with her about this openness to others that she doesn't just act impulsively. When she sees a person in need, she wrestles with God, asking Him what she should do—what *He* wants to do through her. It doesn't come out of her own arrogance that she has something to give these people. She asks God what He wants her to do. She asks how she can love, serve, even die. When God makes that clear to her, she does it. She's not crazy or irrational. She's living a life of more.

REFLECT

Dear children, let us not love with words or speech but with actions and in truth. (1 John 3:18)

It's in Christ that we find out who we are and what we are living for. (Ephesians 1:11, MSG)

What do you think about your new job—loving others? What do the people closest to you need from God today? How is He asking you to meet that need?

 REMEMBER

Each day, remember your job is to love, which means to serve, which means to die to what you want in order to give people what they need, which is a touch from God. Start close in with those nearest and dearest to you.

CHAPTER 10

From Next to Now

W hatever you do, don't miss . . ." Has anyone ever said that to you?

We live focused on the future. Our worries and anxieties, while sometimes based on regrets about the past, tend to be about what is ahead, the big and small details of each day: a meeting with a boss or client, getting your bills paid, a crucial conversation with your spouse or child.

Some of our worries for the future are about the big questions of life: Will I meet someone to marry? Will I have children? Will my marriage last? Will my kids turn out all right? Will I have a good job? Will I have enough money to retire? Will I be healthy?

We keep on asking what's next, what's around the corner, what will happen next week, next year, or in a decade. We rarely label this for what it is: a lack of trust. We call it being responsible.

In worrying about what is next, instead of being grateful for what is now, you miss something very important. You miss your life. Because your life is right now, in the present moment. Whatever you do, don't miss your life.

A Life of More

So far, I have talked about how people live a life of more: it begins with giving up the Kingdom of Me and surrendering to God's love and living in His kingdom, with stepping out of the box. That can be hard, but it makes sense to us on a gut level. If we believe God is all-powerful and loving, then trusting Him makes sense.

The shifts we've made in our quest are similarly logical, even if they are hard to actually do: we move from in the box to out (our kingdom to God's) and learn to say we're sorry; we move from "me" to "we" as we learn to "be still and know" God. We shift from our heads to our hearts as we eat something good every day from God's Word. We move from closed to open as we build a web of relationships and community. We shift from trying to fill ourselves to emptying ourselves and discover the paradox of just how meaningful it is to love, serve, and die. These shifts in our thoughts and actions move us toward a life that is truly life.

The essential thing that holds all these together is something people often don't label as "spiritual," but it is profoundly so. We must develop a new view of time.

Time? Wait, really? Yes. The final shift we need to make that holds everything else together is the shift from next to now. We must change how we view time. How we trust God, how we love others, whether we think we have time to pray, read God's Word, or serve others—all are shaped by our view of time.

A life of more is lived in the moment, trusting God to handle the future. Those living a life of more love God and love people right now, in the moment. They're increasingly free from anxiety and fear and distraction. They don't need to know what's next; they only need to know who is in charge of what's next and be in relationship with Him.

When we look back at our past, we will see a string of moments. Individual encounters with people or things in the created world that happened sequentially, one after the other. If you're like me, you wish you could go back and change some of those moments because of the pain you endured or caused. At the same time, there are moments full of beauty and joy that you wish you could relive in high definition, over and over again.

Life is lived one day at a time, one moment at a time, one decision at a time. Yet when we think about today or even tomorrow, we usually occupy our minds with the lists of things that must be done next, of problems that have to be solved. And with our heads full of all those worries, we miss living in the moment happening now.

Our worries and anxieties are the tattered remnants of a life in the Kingdom of Me. Back there, we believed this awful lie: if we didn't think about all those things, no one else would. The truth is, our Father has already figured out the things that are necessary for our life. We are to focus on today because He has everything else covered. Focus on now, not next.

So what's the shift in our actions we must make in order to live in the now and not in the next? I think it's been described as practicing the presence of God, or living in the present moment. For me, remembering the phrase "slow down to be with" is most helpful. Slow down so that you don't miss the moment, miss your life, miss a life of more. We must go slower and, at that saner, gentler pace, engage with and love people.

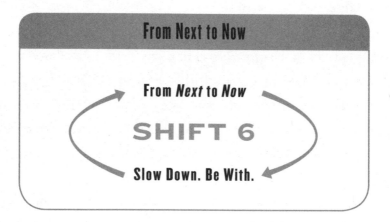

This is the only way we can love another. It is the only way we can live intimately with God. There is no shortcut. Living any other way is a waste of your time and will not lead to life that is truly life. How can we do this? If we want to know what a life guided each moment by God looks like, the best place to look is in God's Word.

How God's People Live in the Now

In the Old Testament, we read story after story of people who lived in the now. When God led the children of Israel out of captivity and slavery in Egypt, He did not present them with a strategic plan or even a map. He led them with a pillar of cloud by day and a pillar of fire by night. If the cloud hovered over the tabernacle, they were supposed to stay. When it moved, they packed up and moved on (see Exodus 13:21–22).

They didn't think about eight steps forward; they simply lived in the now of each day. They let God lead their lives. They let God worry about providing for and protecting them and figuring out what was the best next step for them. They lived in the now, or at least that was the design.

Along the way they sometimes complained or let fear get the best of them. But God always responded with protection and provision: parting the sea, raining down manna (and quail), speaking to Moses on the mountaintop.

Today, we don't have a pillar of cloud or a pillar of fire. That might make for some impressive special effects, but we've got something that is better: the Holy Spirit. The Spirit can guide us in each moment and lead us to do whatever God has for us right now. Jesus lived in this way, and following His example is a great way to live in the now. God is still ready and able to protect and provide, if we can slow down and just trust Him.

"Ruthlessly Eliminate Hurry"

My friend John Ortberg, whom I had the privilege of working with at Willow Creek for almost a decade, recalls a time when he asked his spiritual mentor, Dallas Willard, what he needed to do to be spiritually healthy.

Dallas wisely replied, "You must ruthlessly eliminate hurry from your life." John said, "Okay, that sounds good, what else?" (not noticing that he asked it in a rather hurried manner!). There was a moment of silence and Dallas simply said, "There is nothing else."

It can't be just that, right? There must be some other secret to spiritual health and depth. But this is the truth: adding more spiritual activities to your life will do nothing if you're living at a hurried, frantic pace. You have to slow down. You have to be with God and with people.

I remember when John first told me about that conversation, more than ten years ago. I thought, *Yeah, that's a nice pleasant idea, but I don't have time for that. That's a lovely idea for a wise old man to have and pass down to somebody else, but it's not practical.* However, a decade later, I realize that Dallas was right. Eliminating hurry is the secret to the spiritual life because it enables you to be with God and be with others, to abide fully with God and respond out of the fullness of His love to love other people.

The truth is we can never go fast enough to provide and protect and get everything done that is necessary to ultimately secure our future and to take care of ourselves and to take care of those we love. We can never go fast enough, and we can never check off enough items on a to-do list.

So we might as well slow down and live the moments trusting our future and trusting things to God. Anytime we feel like we need to speed up, that we need to go faster, that is a clue that we're back to living in the box. We might create an illusion of being safe and in control, but we are actually missing our lives. We are missing the joy that comes from gratefully trusting God and seeing Him provide in ways that exceed our expectations.

My wife says to our children (and me), "Don't be in a hurry so you don't have to worry." We say that around our family a lot. I think it would be equally true, but not as rhythmic, to say, "Don't be in a hurry so you don't miss your life."

What if you stopped pushing so hard? What might happen if you stopped pushing people to go faster, whether it's kids putting on their coats, or a work colleague who's explaining a problem, or wanting your spouse to get off the phone so you can tell him or her something, or even just wanting the driver in front of you to go, already, the light is green!

Push kills your life. I push so that things happen at the pace I want them to happen, not at the pace that God would like them to happen. And God has a pace in mind for things, which will bless me. When I push, it destroys the moment. Pushing is a red flag that tells you that you are not living a life of more. When you are feeling the need to push, you are destroying the moment.

I jokingly once told a friend that I might write a book someday and simply title it *Push*. The subtitle would be "How to Ruin Your Life." Because I recall so many times where I've hurt my wife or my children or my friends by not seeing them fully and understanding what they needed from me in the moment because I was going too fast. I was pushing. I was not slowing down. I was not *being with*.

God is gently teaching me to recognize that instinct to push and challenging me to cultivate the ability to stop pushing, to slow down, to reconnect with God, to reconnect to the moment and the people I'm with, and to reconnect with what God wants me to do in that moment. And in that place, I've discovered my life. I've discovered the gifts that God has for me in that moment, the direction He has for me in that moment, so that I don't miss it.

Try this little exercise. Think about the previous week (or month). Ask yourself, *What percentage of time did I live fully present to the moment? Do I have any regrets?*

If I'm honest with myself and there was a real gauge showing me how fully present I was in the sixteen or seventeen hours I'm awake every day, I would be shocked, embarrassed, and undone by that analysis.

This is not about shame but self-awareness. Asking this question at the end of each day can be a great spiritual practice. Before you go to sleep, ask yourself, *What percentage of my day did I live fully present before God and the people He put in my life?* And conversely, *What percentage did I live thinking about what's next?*

I've found this gentle review to be a helpful practice. I simply think through the interactions I had with all the people in my life, whether it was the repairman who fixed a window in my house or the woman at the library who helped me find a room to write this chapter, or whether it's the conversation I had with my wife on the phone or the meeting I was in with four colleagues. As I review my day I simply ask God to show me if I was fully present or if I was zoning out, daydreaming, thinking about what was next, thinking about how ridiculous a conversation was or why I was in this room or what I was going to have for dinner or lunch. Most of us have grown up thinking that pushing through things to get a lot accomplished is the hallmark of success, or even a means of pleasing God. I'm not so sure about that anymore. Sometimes we try to rationalize and say that we're pushing through or doing things God wants us to do. I don't think God ever asks us to do anything that makes us violate the moment, steamroll over people, or miss the opportunity to extend His love and presence to people around us.

In each interaction, ask God what He wants to show you or tell you in that moment. Live so that every moment is an encounter that has meaning. Believe that God is actually directing your steps for a purpose. Trust that each moment is profound no matter how mundane it might appear to you. God wastes no moment. Each moment where you are fully present is a gift.

When we are fully present, not rushing past our lives, we are able to pay attention to promptings and to respond to them. We're able to listen to God and to the people around us. Don't miss those promptings, those whispers from God. I look back at my life, and many times a prompting from God led me to do or say something that turned out to have huge consequences for my life. If you find yourself wondering why you don't hear from God or why He seems distant, look at the pace of your life. Are you missing moments because you are simply running right past them? Whatever you do, don't miss those moments. Slow down enough to pay attention to God and what He's telling you in each moment. Have the trust and courage to act on what He tells you, even when you don't fully understand it.

In order to "be with" others, we need to shift from seeing others as distractions or interruptions to seeing them as people God is using to speak to us. We're not doing them a favor by listening or engaging; we're opening up space to listen to God. Our job is to be with others, to connect with them, to listen to their stories, and to try to ask God in each of those moments, *God, what do You want me to learn from this moment? What is it that You want me to do in this moment? How can I extend Your love in this moment? How can I bless this person in this moment?*

How Jesus Lived

Jesus taught His followers (including us): "Therefore do not worry about tomorrow, for tomorrow will worry about itself. Each day has enough trouble of its own" (Matthew 6:34). Letting tomorrow worry about itself is not easy. But Jesus not only asks us to live this way; He actually put this into practice. He was fully present with people. He saw interruptions as divine appointments and never seemed to be in a hurry.

Jesus talked about being one with the Father, being intimately connected to Him. He encourages us to abide in Him in the same way. He was fully present in each moment, whether it was responding to the woman at the well, walking along the road and calling Zacchaeus out of a tree, or seizing a teachable moment with His disciples when they argued over who was the greatest. He was fully present whether He was with a wealthy man, a religious leader, a fisherman, a Samaritan woman, or a tax collector. He was fully present to everybody, and He lived moment by moment. He moved on and responded only when God asked Him to; He responded to the promptings of God's Spirit.

He did more than just live one day at a time; He lived one moment at a time. He lived in the now. He was fully present with God and with people. He was intimately connected to the Father and did and said what the Father asked Him to do and say. He was completely dialed in to both God and other people in each moment of His day. He invites us to live in the same unhurried manner. When we slow down, we can trust, we can be grateful, we can be with people fully. We won't miss our lives.

WHAT ARE WE AFRAID OF?

Years ago, I wrote in my journal:

It's clear that God has been directing my steps all along. But it's hard for me to rest in that, to fully lean into God completely, to anchor my faith. In order for me to be free to live the kind of life I was designed to live I have to let go of tomorrow. Tomorrow is not real in many ways. The key is to let go of it, to let go of needing it to turn out in certain ways. Jesus makes it very clear the key is to seek first the kingdom of heaven and His righteousness and all of these things will be added to you. But I get overwhelmed by all the uncertainty. This process has exposed how weak my faith really is. I don't say that in shame; it's just a fact. I'm scared a lot, frightened, and have a spirit of fear, but being with God is the safest place to be.

I share these struggles to remind you that I'm just as much of a mess as anyone else. And as I look back on all those years of anxiety and worry and rushing, I realize that I was really just trying to protect and provide for my kingdom.

When you live in the Kingdom of Me, anxiety will be your companion. But if you slow down and pay attention, that companion can be a warning: you've drifted back into the Kingdom of Me. And it's time to step back into God's kingdom and say good-bye to anxiety. It's time to live one day at a time, fully alive and present.

There is an interesting passage in the book of James. He wrote,

Look here, you who say, "Today or tomorrow we are going to a certain town and will stay there a year. We will do business there and make a profit." How do you know what your life will be like tomorrow? Your life is like the morning fog—it's here a little while, then it's gone. What you ought to say is, "If the Lord wants us to, we will live and do this or that." (4:13–15, NLT)

I just love that. We don't know what tomorrow looks like. To think we do is tremendous folly. Who could have predicted that 9/11 would happen? I remember dropping my daughter off at preschool that morning. Lynn called me and said something just happened in New York City. At the office, I sat with some colleagues in front of a television set and watched the towers crumble to the ground. Life as we knew it changed for our country. In a moment, things change. In the moment I got my cancer diagnosis, my life changed. In a moment, life can change unpredictably. If you want another story of how true that is, read the story of my friend Joe in the sidebar on page 186.

Now, I don't mention 9/11 or cancer to make you feel afraid but to remind you that all the worrying, planning, and thinking about the future can't change anything. Our attempts to control are a waste of effort. I'm not saying we should be foolish or reckless, but we should simply trust that God will be with us in every moment—happy or sad, joyful or scary.

Trust me; I'm not suggesting you become a slacker and ignore your responsibilities. I have a will. I have a financial plan. I still need to prepare for things in advance. Living in the moment doesn't mean you quit looking ahead completely. It's really a matter of balance and priorities. Keep everything in God's perspective. There's a phrase we often use in business that not everyone appreciates: "Work smarter, not harder." Some of our rushing around is unnecessary; we bring it on ourselves by procrastinating on the one hand or overplanning on the other. If you leave everything until the last minute, you're always going to be in a rush. But you can also spend way too much time planning, reviewing your plan, revising your plan, taking another look at it. Give it a rest. All that "stuff" is not the source of your joy and peace. Give it only the priority it deserves. Slow down. Be with.

Remember, Jesus said, "Don't be anxious about tomorrow" (see Philippians 4:6).

Joe's Story

Three years ago on an extended vacation, I decided to spend a couple of hours every morning just praying, journaling, and reading the Bible. I was earnestly asking what it means to walk with Jesus. John 15 is about abiding and I wondered what that looks like. Dallas Willard writes that the kingdom of God is available, here and now, but you have to want it more than anything else—which means letting go of everything. And I thought, *What if I wanted this?*

My wife and I began to pray: *God, everything we have is on the table. Nothing is off-limits. You can have it all.* Not long after that, my position was eliminated. It was hard and felt unfair, but I really think it was God's way of answering our prayers. I gave Him my job, and He took it.

WHAT TO DO NOW?

We cannot slow down when we are focused on any time besides the present moment. Most of us tend to feel rushed when we're worried about the future—even when "the future" is only a few hours away on a busy day. When I feel worried or anxious about the future, I simply ask myself this question: *Do I know what to do now?*

When I've asked myself that question I've always known the answer. I've always known what to do now. First thing in the morning, when I'm in the shower thinking about the day, I can easily start

I found another job, and well, it wasn't a great fit. And I thought, *Okay, when I surrender like this, I'm going to see fruit.* But it wasn't that easy. I don't think I've ever been more yielded, surrendered, tender, even on the verge of tears a lot of the time—yet never been less fruitful, at least in the way I understood it.

So I prayed, *God, You said You would bear fruit. I don't see any fruit. I don't understand.* I sensed God saying, *You think fruit is about what you do, and I think fruit is about who you are. Abiding in Me is not about performance. It's about you living moment by moment with Me.*

As I began to embrace that, I got a call from an old friend who said he had an open position and he knew I was the perfect fit. And so far, it seems pretty perfect. Only God.

thinking about what I've got to get done and I get a bit anxious, because people are depending on me and there is a chance something will slip through the cracks. Then I catch myself and ask, *Do I know what to do now?* The answer is, *Yes, finish my shower.* Easy enough. Then after that moment I know what to do now: eat some breakfast. Then I need to get to work and prepare for meetings or whatever I need to do. In each moment it seems like I know what to do now, and next takes care of itself. I've done this for the past three years, and it has changed my relationship with God and with the people around me. It has shifted my thinking from next to now. It has set me free from much of my anxiety.

Sometimes we really don't know what to do right now. In those moments, we need to reconnect with God and ask, *What do You want me to do right now in this moment?* We'll be guided by His Spirit; we'll be guided from the truth of His words to know how to respond in the moment right now. That's His promise to us. If we slow down and be with God, He will guide us.

We may not know what to do for the next week or month or year, but we usually know what to do right now, in the moment we're in. When we don't know, God does, and He's right there with us, ready to guide.

Yes, you have a report to prepare for a meeting next month, but your daughter wants to read you her book report. Do you know what to do right now?

You have one of those difficult one-on-ones with a direct report on Friday, but for some reason you've been thinking about a friend of yours who's waiting for the results of a biopsy. Do you know what to do right now?

You have all sorts of things that need to be done tomorrow and the next day and the next, but God has just one phone call for you to make, one word of comfort to offer, one embrace to share right now. Do you really believe Jesus when He says tomorrow will take care of tomorrow?

When we shift our thoughts from next to now and shift our actions by slowing down and being with God and with people, we will never miss our life. Instead, we'll discover the life that is truly life, which God wants to give us right now.

REFLECT

Whether you turn to the right or to the left, your ears
will hear a voice behind you, saying, "This is the way;
walk in it." (Isaiah 30:21)

But the Advocate, the Holy Spirit, whom the Father
will send in my name, will teach you all things and
will remind you of everything I have said to you.
(John 14:26)

Think about your relationship with speed. Do you like to go fast?
Why? What do you think about people who go slow?

REMEMBER

Each day, focus on what's happening right now instead of worrying about what's next. Slow down to be with God and others. Do not miss your life.

f we're going to talk about life, we have to understand death.

That may seem counterintuitive. But if you've read this far, you may have noticed that I keep bringing up death, which is mildly ironic since I'm writing about the life that is truly life. Airplanes falling from the sky, a cancer diagnosis, backyard epiphanies about dying to self—I realize these stories might make this sound like a book about death. In fact, in chapter 9 I said our shift in action is captured by the phrase "love, serve, and die." But as you've hopefully begun to see, embracing this paradox is the first step toward living a life of more.

What must die is our false self. In order to live in the reality that God offers us, not just someday in heaven but right now, we must decide to put to death something that is good so that we can have what is best. And that "good but not best" thing is a life in which we run things and have a little of God when we need Him to help us out. That's life in the Kingdom of Me, with a bit of God.

The problem with that, as we've seen, is that a life with "just enough God" is not how life was supposed to be, because it really is a choice between life and death. If we choose that, we may think we're saying yes to a little bit of God in our box, but that choice really means we are saying no to the life God has planned for us right here and now. It's saying, "I'll wait until later to get that." But in so doing, we will miss everything He has for us, everything He wants to do. We kill God's vision for why He created us to begin with, and we let that dream die.

Why would we miss out on that when God offers us so much more? Why not choose life right now? Why not respond right now to God's calling to come outside our box, to be raised from the dead like Lazarus was, and to live fully this life He has given us? The path to life is the death of the false self.

Helen Keller once said, "Life is either a daring adventure or nothing."* But we must choose to begin the daring adventure by getting out of the box. You have to accept it's an all-or-nothing proposition. It's not just a little bit of God to have a little better life. You either have your life or you don't have your life. It's a choice we must make.

WE'RE AT A CROSSROADS

There is a verse in the Old Testament in which God, after explaining what following Him would look like and what it would mean to be His people, offers a challenge to the children of Israel, His chosen people: "This day I call the heavens and the earth as witnesses against you that I have set before you life and death, blessings and curses.

---

* Helen Keller, *Let Us Have Faith* (New York: Doubleday, 1940), 51.

Now choose life, so that you and your children may live and that you may love the LORD your God, listen to his voice, and hold fast to him. For the LORD is your life" (Deuteronomy 30:19–20).

If we have a choice between life and death, between blessings and curses, wouldn't we choose life and blessings? But the thing is, we don't. Because to live the life that is truly life, we have to die to self. We have to die to the idea that we can have God as an accessory in the Kingdom of Me. And when we die to that idea, we can choose life, and we'll find that everything is waiting for us, that we now have access to everything that God wants to give us, the life that is truly life.

Throughout the pages of Scripture, God invites us into this new life:

That means you must not give sin a vote in the way you conduct your lives. Don't give it the time of day. Don't even run little errands that are connected with that old way of life. Throw yourselves wholeheartedly and full-time— remember, you've been raised from the dead!—into God's way of doing things. Sin can't tell you how to live. After all, you're not living under that old tyranny any longer. You're living in the freedom of God. (Romans 6:12–14, MSG)

At the crossroads, choose to live in the freedom of God. You will find contentment and joy, and the people around you will also discover that their lives are changed by yours.

Do It for the Kids

Maybe you're scared or you think, *I'm good. I'm with God, but I've worked hard to build a life and I'm not really ready to give it up. God's helping me with my kingdom, and I like that. That life of more sounds exciting but way too hard.*

If you can't find enough motivation within yourself to make that choice, then I want to appeal to you to choose the life that is truly life for the sake of those closest to you: your spouse, your children, your friends, your family, because they need you to live this kind of life.

Your spouse is looking for a life-giving marriage. I know this is what my wife is looking for. After more than twenty years of marriage Lynn knows when I'm at my best and when I'm not. Sometimes she will just ask, with love and courage, "Where are you? There is more inside of you, but it seems like you're frozen."

For years I would resist those conversations, especially that question: Where are you? Because the answer, as it was when God asked Adam and Eve the same question in the garden, is "I'm hiding" (see Genesis 3:10).

So sometimes, in those conversations, I would go to default, to my box. I would hide. "No, not really, I'm fine," I'd tell my wife. But as God worked on my heart I began to live into her question and admit, even if I didn't use those words, that I was hiding. I realize hiding is the way of death. I realize that what she really needs from me is life, which is something I can't give her on my own.

However, when I choose to live a life of more, the life that is really life, I can give her something precious: a touch from God Himself. She, our children, and my friends need for me to be filled with God enough to give that away to them. To love my wife, my children, and my friends with God's love. That's what she needs. That's what my children need. And that's what the people you love need as well.

JUST START

Three years ago my family moved from the Chicago suburbs to the outskirts of San Antonio. In many ways, that move was catalyzed by this book—and my own desire for more. It was becoming clear that my calling to help lead one local church was ending and a new calling, a broader calling, was emerging, which included writing this book. A new home, a new job, a new church community, new schools for the children—we made big adjustments.

A month after settling into our new house, I was heating something up in the microwave. I took a few moments to respond to its beeping insistence that I remove my breakfast. As I approached the machine, in green letters it declared, "Press Start for More." I was in the midst of working on this book—and struggling with it, to understate it. And now, even the microwave was reminding me to write it! In fact, I did not want to write this book; I wished someone else would write it—anyone but me. I thought about "more" all the time, but I felt stuck. I stared at that digital message again: "Press Start for More," and my immediate thought was, *I wish it was that easy.* I wish all I had to do to write this book was press Start. But if I could, what would "Start" look like?

Well, for three years I have seen that same phrase, "Press Start for More," taunting me, saying, "It's easy. Just press Start." As if. Those thoughts led to self-doubt: *Why do you need to write a book about a life of more? Besides, who are you to tell people how to live? And what does "start" look like?*

As much as I didn't want to, I *had* to write this book. And not just because of the message on the microwave! There were times I didn't want to, but the book (and God) would not let me go. I felt compelled to write it, even when I felt reluctant to do so. Not because I have it all figured out and you need to hear all the things I have learned. No. I had to do this because I had connected deeply with the longing and desire expressed by five hundred thousand people who told our research team what they wanted from God and their church. The data collected through a survey, together with hundreds of individual conversations, confirmed that people were longing for more *and* that they were starting to give up hope that it existed this side of heaven. But others had found that life of more. They were living it, here and now. And I needed to share what those people had discovered with the thousands who were still searching.

I tried to run from this assignment many times, thinking it was someone else's job to tell this story. But I could not get those voices out of my head, and they were permanently attached to my heart. I had to let you know that you are not alone and you are not crazy in wanting more. You are made to have more and it is possible *now*.

You. Are. Not. Crazy. You believe that a life of more is out there somewhere; you long for it. You're not crazy, because such a life is possible. And you are not alone, because thousands of people are living that life every day. It is the life you were made to live. It is the life I am eager to live and even more eager to share with you.

If it is not evident to you yet, I am very much in process—a process that is messy and incomplete. I am very much on this journey with you. I have good days when I am living with God outside the box, experiencing freedom, peace, and a fullness of life. And then there are days, many days, that I spend living in the dark shadows of my tiny little cardboard world where the air is stale and I am not present to God or anybody in my life.

But I am living increasingly more of my days with God, in His kingdom, and I have a new hope deep within my soul. A hope and belief that God is taking care of all the details of my life, that He wants to do every moment of every day with me, that He is transforming me to be more loving, starting with those who are most dear to me—my wife and children.

And then one morning, when the microwave again reminded me that I needed to press Start, it was clear. I did just have to start—to turn the passion in my heart into words on a page. And you, the one longing to live a life of more, also need to just start. Of course, after that first step, the journey is long, messy, complicated, and has many ups and downs, but starting is easy. You simply must decide that you want a life of more. That desire is enough. The rest happens one step at a time. You must start. That's all God needs because He's the One who is guiding and directing your journey.

You were made for more, and more is possible. Knowing that, you can't unlearn it. Now it's your decision. Are you going to start? It's messy and complicated yet simple at the same time.

In chapter 2, I told you about my unusual childhood introduction to opera and, in particular, the classic Italian opera *Turandot*. As you may recall, the title character is a beautiful princess with an ice-cold heart. Calaf, a prince in exile, falls for Turandot at first sight. He's willing to risk everything, even his life, to pursue the possibility of living a life of more—a life with Turandot. To win her heart, and her hand, suitors must answer three riddles, believed to be too difficult for anyone. If he fails, he will die. It's an all-or-nothing proposition. But having seen Turandot, having caught a glimpse of what could be, Calaf cannot go back to his pretty good, ordinary life as a prince. He wants more. There is no turning back.

In the opera, Calaf marks his decision to accept the challenge of the riddles (and winning Turandot's hand) by banging a gong. He is declaring, to himself and everyone else, that he is willing to risk it all for love.

He bangs the gong. In a way, he presses Start so that he can live a life of more. Or die trying. He bangs the gong, telling everyone: I am willing to die in order to get that which I desire. There's no going back.

So what about you? Are you ready for more? I hope you know by now that it is possible. Really possible, right now.

You need to bang the gong.

You need to declare, *Yes, God, I want more. More of You. I'm willing to let my old life go in order to pursue a life of more.* And then you will find yourself taking the first step outside of your own box, leaving your own kingdom to follow, moment by moment, the One who has loved you from the beginning. The One who will never, ever fail you. The One who can fill you with true life and give you what you desire above all else, which is love.

A life of more means letting go of the life of less. You'll have to risk letting the life of less die. Your life of less might be pretty good, but once you know there's more and that real people are actually experiencing it, you need to be willing to take that step. Will you turn your back on the life you have now (which is okay but full of that nagging feeling that there's got to be more) and trust that God will meet you and give you the life you've always wanted, the real desire of your heart? When you make that decision, it's powerful.

So it comes to this: What do you want? An ordinary life with some of God, or life itself?

The mallet's in your hand, the gong is in front of you, and you need to decide.

Bang the gong.

Acknowledgments

Writing is mostly a solitary experience, but writing and publishing a book takes a small village. God used these folks to breathe life into me throughout the creative process, and for that I am incredibly grateful.

To my wife, Lynn, and our children: Jackson, Aubrey, and John. Your belief in me and this message, along with your timely advice, made all the difference in the world. This book would not have been written without their very tangible expressions of love.

To Eric Arnson, Terry Schweizer, and Cally Parkinson, my partners in research for over a decade. None of this would be possible without their efforts to understand how spiritual growth works.

To Bob Buford and the Bob, Inc. team of Todd Wilson, Doug Slaybaugh, and Derek Bell, who believed I had something to say and supported the development of the first draft.

To Lyn Cryderman, who early on polished my words. I am particularly grateful for the moment when he looked up from his computer and said, "I think you're talking about the Kingdom of Me."

To Keri Wyatt Kent for helping me cross the finish line, providing much-needed writing and editing assistance. Her partnership was invaluable.

To Randy Frazee, my friend and colleague at Oak Hills, who championed this book in hundreds of selfless ways.

To Steve Green, my friend and agent, who led me through the publishing process and convinced me I had something to say.

To Max Lucado for writing the foreword and for creating a culture at Oak Hills that values the written word.

To Jim Barker, friend and Oak Hills elder, for spending hours and hours helping me understand that the goal is oneness and it starts right now.

To Brett Eastman, my dear friend, who at the start said, "The title is obvious. It's *More*."

To Scott Gibson and Don Wink, my dear friends and integral members of my "web," for their over-the-top belief in me.

To Praveen Kommu, whose teachable spirit and willing heart allowed me to test my theories about how someone pursues intimacy with God.

To Sam, Joe, and Scott for sharing their stories with me (and you).

To John Blase, my editor, for his ever-present advocacy and expertise. I could not imagine a better partner.

To Alex Field, Amy Haddock, Beverly Rykerd, and the rest of the WaterBrook Multnomah team for their wholehearted support.

To Gateway Worship and Bethel Music, whose worship music served as the soundtrack for my writing.

And to Skip, my dad. "You're the reason why the opera is in me."* I love you.

---

* U2, "Sometimes You Can't Make It on Your Own," released November 17, 2004, on *How to Dismantle an Atomic Bomb,* Interscope Records.